Small Business Branding 101

BIANCA VAN DER MEULEN

ISBN: 9781072163633

CONTENTS

ACKNOWLEDGMENTS

Raising a baby, branding a business, and writing a book—each takes a village, at least to do it well.

This book would not exist without Mara Measor, my best friend, business partner, and cover artist. Your tireless work and gentle realism have kept my feet on the ground and our agency moving forward.

Thanks to my loved ones who made writing a book in my third and fourth trimester possible—David, Louise, and Doña Marina. You took care of me so I could take care of my book baby and my human baby at the same time.

Many thanks to my editors and proofreaders—Hendrik, Elias, and Alicia. Your input turned a pile of raw material into a presentable piece of content.

A very special thanks to the entrepreneurs we've worked with. Our projects are what motivate, inspire, and teach me day-to-day. To Jen, Jess, and Yohanes, especially—thank you for letting me use your stories to help others. It's that kind of collaboration and generosity that makes small business great.

INTRODUCTION

When I sat down to write this book, the nerd and the business owner within me were at war. The nerd, a passionate teacher and psychology junkie, wanted everyone to know about the fascinating history of branding, the interesting interplay of economics and psychology, the conflicting marketing philosophies that have mingled over time to create a beautifully messy backdrop to each unique brand...

"Ain't nobody got time for that!" the business owner shouted. "Do you have any idea how many things are on our to-do list today? Just explain how to build a freaking brand—as quickly and clearly as you can, please!"

This tension is one reason it's very difficult to find high-quality content and advice for small business owners. Nerds are thinkers. They tend to invest in formal education, develop niche expertise, and end up in large organizations with salaries and the freedom to focus on what they do best. Small business owners are doers. They tend to figure things out as they go along, embrace being a jack of all trades, and prefer the freedom to build an enterprise around their interests and values.

After freelance writing for small companies over four years and working with over 100 entrepreneurs as co-owner of a boutique

9

agency, I've been on both sides of the equation. I understand how difficult it is (as a nerd) to provide thoughtful services to a market perpetually strapped for cash. I also understand how frustrating it is (as a small business owner) to get advice from a "business expert" who doesn't get your business. Some consultants have an MBA, decades of corporate experience, and no knowledge of the day-to-day challenges of being an entrepreneur.

This war is why Small Business Branding 101 is written the way it is. You're a business owner; your brand is not hypothetical. Every new idea has practical implications—which is why this book is full of exercises, examples, and hands-on applications. Welcome to your crash course in branding.

HOW TO READ THIS BOOK

This book is designed to satisfy both the nerd and the business owner in you.

Part I: Building A Strong(er) Brand introduces branding theory that filters theoretical and real-world branding expertise through the lens of small business. It also introduces the Brand Canvas, a one-page tool you'll use to create clarity about your brand.

Part II: Create Your Own Brand Canvas is the meat of Small Business Branding 101. It gives you step-by-step instructions for how to capture your unique, crystal-clear brand identity using a Brand Canvas. This section is more of a workbook than a casual read. So be prepared to roll up your sleeves! Each section includes a case study, an explanation, an example (from Sunbird Creative's own Brand Canvas), exercises, and key takeaways.

The **Glossary** is a quick reference guide to branding and marketing terms as used in this book, refined on the frontlines of small business.

How you approach this material depends on your goal. If you're just curious, you're welcome to simply read the book straight through. You'll get some food for thought and a fresh take on branding.

If you're looking for hands-on learning that results in new clarity about your brand and how to improve it, prepare for a more intensive experience. Here's how to get the most out of this book and walk away with a complete big-picture view of your brand:

1. Read Part I for some branding theory and an orientation to the Brand Canvas.

2. Gather a few resources: a notebook or computer, quiet space and time to think, and a blank Brand Canvas (digital or hard copy). Templates and sample Brand Canvas documents are available at sunbirdcreative.com/

    a. branding-101-book

3. Dive into Part II. Doing the exercises as you read each section will help you capture your thoughts while they're fresh.

4. Once you're done reading and completing the exercises, you'll fill out your Brand Canvas document!

WHY I WROTE THIS BOOK

Ten years ago, I would not have called myself "entrepreneurial" or agreed that businesses can do good. I certainly never intended to become a brand strategist for small businesses. In fact, nothing was further from my mind. The very thought would have made me gag.

My father worked for the federal government and my mother was an elementary school teacher. The thought of making money selling products or services was never breathed in our home. The only commentary I ever heard on business was my mom complaining that one of the private schools she worked for "runs like a business"— by which she meant that it was self-centered and greedy. As a creative, idealistic person growing up in a household where finances and entrepreneurship were never talked about, I grew up with the vague idea that money was dirty.

I graduated New York University in 2011, three years after the start of the Great Recession, with a degree in English and American Literature. The fact that I had graduated summa cum laude did not at all ease my suspicion that I wouldn't "make it" in the "real world," where my generation was the first in America that was going to be worse off than their parents. Still, I was determined to find my own way. At the time this meant avoiding corporate jobs on the one hand and finding my calling on the other. This risky optimism was the beginning of what I would now call my entrepreneurial journey.

Finding my own way looked like trying out a dozen different jobs that had absolutely nothing to do with my degree. I became a math teacher, a nanny, a kung fu instructor, an administrative assistant, a guest services rep, a tutor... I challenged myself to give every job my full attention and best effort. The unintended consequence of this effort was that I mastered each job quickly and got bored.

Slowly, I gave in to the idea that I'd have to find a way to use my writing skills and literature degree if I was going to make money, be taken seriously, and be happy. So I Googled "how to become a freelance writer," set up a personal website, and created profiles on writer associations and job matchmaking platforms.

Once again, I was entering a new world. It took me months just to figure out what to name the services I provided as an independent writer/editor. But I quickly made double, then triple, what I was making at my "real" jobs. I got good at finding projects I knew I'd excel at and pitching myself successfully in a sea of competitors.

And once again I did it my way: Instead of picking a super-specialized niche within a field (the most common way to stand out and become profitable as a freelance writer), I found a niche that actually tapped into my range of abilities (as a writer, editor, and researcher), fulfilled my desire for variety (in subject matter), and created real benefit for a set of clients I actually enjoyed working with (small business owners). My niche was writing long-form, jargon-free educational blog content. I wrote like an expert on finance, law, nutrition, exercise science, and business in a way that connected the real experts to their audiences. I got really good at taking on the persona of my clients and speaking for them in a way that made their readers trust and learn from them.

Sometimes the implications of my role scared me. Who was I to give financial advice to thousands of readers? I didn't even have a credit card! (Apparently banks aren't jumping to extend credit to self-employed writers with part-time minimum-wage jobs.)

Throughout this time, I was so wrapped up in trying to find my place in the "real world" that I didn't realize I had landed squarely in the last place I ever thought I would find myself: the business world. As a freelancer, I realized, I was managing a company of one, and virtually all my clients were small business owners.

Even more surprisingly, I had fallen in love. Entrepreneurship—more than teaching, more than writing, and certainly more than administrative assisting—gave me the chance to unite everything I loved: independence, variety, creativity, communication skills, passion, usefulness.

It turned out to be the best of idealism and pragmatism rolled into one. Entrepreneurship—which I consider an umbrella term for any new venture, from a local social enterprise, to a "mom and pop shop," to a well-funded tech startup—is what feeds millions of families, creates solutions to difficult problems, and sometimes grows into massive organizations that touch billions of lives (for better or worse). Entrepreneurship is the heart of successful small business, and it's the best of capitalism.

I realized that I loved entrepreneurial small business owners. I also realized that many of them were on the same journey I was: trying to marry their passions and skills in a way that provided real value to other people. They struggled with the same question: How do you make the money you need to live by doing something you love to do and are good at—while working with people you actually like? It's a bold question.

Just like me at the beginning of my freelance writing career, many of the small business owners I met launched into business with a sense that they had something special to offer the world and confidence that, in time, they would figure out the rest.

But the help that's available along the journey tends to come in only two flavors: inspirational advice and traditional business advice. The first aims to take care of psychological needs, like getting rid of imposter syndrome and holding on to your dreams without feeling defeated. The second aims to teach hard skills every business needs to survive, like bookkeeping and creating operational systems.

Without a doubt, both soft and hard skills are essential to starting and running a successful new venture. The problem is that they rarely overlap, and their language comes from such different worlds, that for people new to business it can feel like they have to make a choice between being idealistic and realistic.

This book is the fruit of three years "on the ground" as a business owner and strategist, doing branding work in the trenches alongside over 100 clients as a co-founder of branding agency Sunbird Creative. Neither I nor my business partner (Mara, our design wizard) had an MBA. We didn't rise through the ranks of a famous creative agency. We started our company in 2015 with three key resources: $3,000 in savings, solid writing/design skills, and firsthand knowledge of the challenges of small business strategy.

What I loved about branding from Day 1 is that it unites both the soft and hard side of business, just as entrepreneurship unites idealism and pragmatism. Unlike mindset coaching on the one hand or bookkeeping on the other, branding challenges you to think about business in a holistic way. Hearts and numbers are intertwined. Not being profitable is a branding problem; so is not being sincere about your values. Going through the branding process requires you to discover who you really are—both powers and limits—and who your customer really is.

In spite of how it's talked about in some business schools, the exchange of goods and services—even in e-commerce—is an extremely personal interaction, full of meanings and emotions. People who are great at branding see business as a human exchange, where the goal is living in a mutual beneficial relationship and the ultimate metric is trust.

I wrote this book because there aren't a lot of voices out there for small business owners who, like me, are idealistic and realistic, creative and pragmatic. Yet this balance is essential for branding effectively and authentically.

This book is dedicated to entrepreneurial souls who know that businesses—no matter how small—have the power to do good. It's a branding guide for ambitious men and women who believe that every enterprise should have higher goals than "penetrating the market" or "dominating the competition." It's for people who want to master the art of marketing but feel uncomfortable describing their customers as consumers. It's for those who understand the importance of being financially savvy but refuse to reduce their clients to dollar signs. In short, this book is for humans.

PART 1:
BUILDING A STRONGER BRAND

You want to create a brand that humans love.

You've heard about 'brand identity' and the importance of it being 'authentic' and 'unique.' You know that mission statements, core values, and brand personalities are pieces of the puzzle. You know that standing out matters, as does having a good logo. In other words, you've got a lot of ideas about branding swirling around in your head.

But what on Earth are you supposed to do?

The reason branding can seem complicated is because, well, it is. Building a brand is an ancient practice that taps into the deepest parts of the human psyche. It's also a contextual practice that requires you to be very aware of the rapidly changing ways people think, communicate with one another, and buy products or services.

But knowing all the history of branding and statistics about consumer behavior is not enough to do branding well. Building a brand is challenging no matter how many facts you know because:

A brand (like a person) is not a single, measurable thing—it's a holistic collection of dynamic elements. This makes branding both extremely fun to do and impossible to master in one go.

The process (like building a meaningful human relationship) is demanding. It requires you to be honest with yourself, face uncomfortable realities, and get creative with your resources. It also requires you to experiment and iterate over time, getting better as you go.

When it comes to branding, as with most important things in life, there's no silver bullet. There are no shortcuts, no formulas, no one 'hack' that will guarantee success. In the end, you have to put your whole self into the process, give it your all and do your best—and you might still not end up with the dream business you originally imagined. But you will create something much more valuable (to you and your customers) than if you had not tried at all.

If these challenges excite as much as scare you, you're in the perfect mindset to succeed at branding—and enjoy the ride. Let's begin!

THE HUMAN BRANDING APPROACH

In an age where you can get 10 high-quality versions of any product shipped to your door within 48 hours, how do you decide what to buy?

This is not a problem people ever had to face before the 21st century. And there are clearly massive implications for businesses. High-quality mass production, the breakneck pace of technological progress, unprecedented access to information (and misinformation), late-stage capitalism, consumerism, social media—these changes affect every aspect of our lives, from how our brains work, to how we make babies, to how we interact with strangers on the other side of the globe.

These technology-driven changes have changed the way we talk and think about branding. At the same time, the basic principles of branding are as old as human nature. The term "human branding" is meant to remind us business owners that our business enterprises are by humans, for humans.

As people, we are deeply attuned to other people. Babies recognize facial features and can identify emotions before their vision is even fully developed. We even project human characteristics onto non-human things: We tend to think of our pets as members of the family; we put googly eyes on inanimate objects; we bond with Mickey Mouse and Mr. Potato Head; we see faces in rock formations. (When I was five or six years old, I drew eyes on a large pebble, named it Lulu, and carried it in my arms like a child for weeks.) In short, we are wired to detect humanity.

That's why the most useful and effective way to think about the complex and abstract concept of a brand is to think of it as human— as a human. When we think of our small business brand as a human being—created by us, similar to us, but not us—we're able to think intuitively and clearly about it. And more importantly, we're able to see it the same way the customers we are trying to reach see it.

Thinking of your brand as a human rather than an abstract concept can give you patience with its growth and help you detect what parts are missing. People are quirky and unique. They have strengths and weaknesses, passions and values. The same goes for brands. If your brand is like a person, you can nurture it, strengthen it, help it thrive in the world. If your brand is like a person, it's easier to accept that not everyone will like it, which frees you to be bold and authentic.

One alternative to the human branding approach is thinking of a brand as a kind of costume, a disguise for the heartless business machinery underneath. This approach misses the beauty of branding and encourages the idea that corporate responsibility is limited to what the law, rather than conscience, dictates.

Another alternative is thinking of a brand as a collection of designs, or words, or products. This approach misses the power of human relationship a business actually holds. Your customers are not just minds attached to wallets, with mental "real estate" for sale. They are a mysterious web of body, heart, mind, and soul. They are navigating the world, as well as their own likes and dislikes, powers and limitations.

Humans buy food and goods and experiences, but they are not only consumers. Humans cook food and make goods and craft experiences, but they are not only providers. We all live within an economy, but we are not only economic units. We are both frighteningly predictable and wildly unpredictable, rational and irrational, intelligent and foolish. Like responsible people, responsible brands respect the humanity of those they interact with.

Clearly, a brand is much more than a name, logo, or product. It's a set of impressions, feelings, and experiences that culminate in a reputation in the real world. A brand is a holistic entity made up of many dynamic elements, all interacting with each other, living in the messiness of the real world—by which I don't mean on shelves or screens. A strong brand is one that's highly specific and that lives in other people's minds. It's a brand that means something real to a number of real, live human beings.

Forgetting that your customers are human leads to two highly damaging flaws in business branding:

1. Over-simplifying the customer
2. Over-complicating the business

The solution is to think about branding as a relationship between two people: your business and your customer. This is the essence of the human branding approach. And it's the framework behind the Brand Canvas, which aims to "flesh out" your brand identity in human terms.

INTRODUCING THE BRAND CANVAS

The idea for the Brand Canvas came out of years of working with small business owners and solopreneurs as a freelance writer. My job was not just to pump out generic content; it was to capture the voice of each client's brand, so that readers were not just informed but also engaged, delighted, and persuaded. At least, that's the bar I set for myself.

As far as branding went, many of my clients gave no direction ("I just need three 500-word blog posts about life insurance"), some gave a little direction ("It needs to be funny... but not too funny"), and none gave me written brand guidelines to follow. So I pieced together an understanding of their personality, tone, and message by interviewing them, combing through their website and marketing materials, and scouring the Internet for customer reviews. Through the process, I was basically creating brand guidelines for each client in my head.

I empathized with my entrepreneurial clients. They loved their work and cared about their business, but most were overwhelmed. They were busy and profitable enough to outsource pieces of their marketing to freelance creatives like me, but they laughed at the idea of hiring an agency or consultant. Spend tens of thousands of dollars

Brand Canvas

	Story	Mission	Values
WHY			
WHAT	Differentiators	Unique Value Proposition	Core Competency
HOW	Style	Brand Persona	Voice
WHO	Psychographics	Demographics	Behaviors

on something as vague as "brand identity"? Forget it.

I realized that there were a few common reasons my clients didn't have brand guidelines to share with their creative team:

1. They saw each marketing campaign and creative asset as independent efforts (rather than opportunities to develop a consistent brand over time)
2. They assumed that a formal branding process was only for big companies with big budgets
3. They wanted to create a brand strategy and guidelines, but were confused by the conflicting or piecemeal advice they found about it
4. They didn't know where to start

As someone who loved research and a challenge, I wanted to find the answer to these challenges for my clients. What I learned was discouraging. Branding is not a formal discipline like mathematics, geology, or even art. There are no hard-and-fast rules. Even multinational brands with decades of history struggle to do it well. It was no wonder that there aren't any simple versions of the branding process accessible to small business owners.

When my friend and graphic designer Mara and I decided to take our partnership from referring clients to each other to working together as one company to address their needs, I saw my opportunity. Now I had both the designer's perspective and the motivation I needed to establish those simple brand guidelines for small business owners I had been itching to create.

In our first year together as Sunbird Creative, I created v1.0 of what we called the "Brand Profile." Like a dating profile, the Brand Profile captured the elements of a business that customers would most care about. This included brand personality but also things like value proposition and core values. As experienced creatives, we knew it was important to see the big picture before talking about the details of design, voice, or even brand personality. Otherwise we'd hear things like, "I would describe my brand personality as no-

nonsense, down-to-earth, professional. The voice should be bold and the logo should feature my favorite color, hot pink."

It was very important to me that the Brand Profile fit on one page. I wanted our clients to see every component of their brand in one glance. I envisioned them tacking it up over their computer, not flipping back and forth between the pages of a massive binder that would inevitably get lost under their desk.

The Brand Profile went through several iterations over the course of three years, reality-tested by over 100 clients. My instinct to keep it one page turned out to be a good one. Entrepreneurs were able to understand how their brand fit in to their business in a new way, and the limited space forced both us and our clients to stick to only the most important concepts. We tried different ways of organizing and naming the brand elements to see what made the most sense to others. We added elements like story as we realized what it needed to be more holistic and removed elements like vision when it was proven too redundant to belong on this one-pager alongside mission.

In those same years, I became enamored with Strategyzer's Business Model Canvas. After spending a significant chunk of our first year writing a 20-page business plan we never used, here was a one-page solution to the messy question of business strategy that actually made sense—for any business. I was thrilled to find out that the Business Model Canvas was being used by cutting-edge tech startups and corporate behemoths alike. Its success validated the Brand Profile in a new way. And inspired us to rename the Brand Profile as the Brand Canvas.

Creating a Brand Canvas for our clients is my favorite part of being a brand strategist. I love seeing small business owners' eyes light up when the thoughts that have been swirling around in their heads for so long appear before them on a single, pristine, totally manageable sheet of paper. It's like watching someone fall in love all over again.

Ultimately, the Brand Canvas is a tool to capture your entire brand identity on one page, making you the expert on your brand and giving you answers to four key questions:

- Who is going to fall in love with your brand?
- Why does your business exist?
- What are your superpowers?
- How does your brand look and sound?

I'm so excited to share this process with you.

The goal of the rest of this book is to help you create your own Brand Canvas. I'll give you examples, exercises, and tips along every step of the way. I've done this process with a huge range of entrepreneurs—from authors to caterers, from product designers to optometrists—and can honestly say that every single one of them benefited from answering the questions and capturing their brand on one page. Most have found it downright enjoyable to take the time to think creatively and strategically about their brand. Several clients have described feeling physically lighter afterward (really!).

By now I think that you know I'm not a fan of overpromising and/or BS. The Brand Canvas is not going to solve all your branding challenges in one shot. But it is a huge first step for anyone on the path to building a stronger, smarter small business brand. That much I can confidently promise you.

PART II:
CREATE YOUR OWN BRAND CANVAS

Now that you know what a Brand Canvas is and why it's incredibly useful for an effective (and human) approach to branding, it's time to create your own.

Before you continue, you'll need a place to keep notes and answer questions—this can be either a computer or old-fashioned notebook. It might also be useful to have a hard copy of the Brand Canvas on hand. You can find blank templates as part of the Brand Canvas Toolkit at www.sunbirdcreative.com/toolkits

The following process can be intense—and a lot of fun. I recommend setting aside a few hours in a favorite spot to tackle the sections one at a time. If you treat this process like an important assignment worthy of your time and full attention, I guarantee you'll discover new and exciting things about yourself and your business.

Let's begin!

WHO

WHY	Story	Mission	Values
WHAT	Differentiators	Unique Value Proposition	Core Competency
HOW	Style	Brand Persona	Voice
WHO	Psychographics	Demographics	Behaviors

Who is going to fall in love with your brand?

The "Who" section of the Brand Canvas paints a picture of your target customer according to three types of characteristics:

- Psychographics
- Demographics
- Behaviors

Knowing exactly what kind of customer is the best fit for your brand gives you a firm foundation for the rest of the branding process.

Clarity about your "Who" is a key element of a strong brand and sustainable business. But it usually takes years to identify, and a lifetime to refine. It's not easy figuring out who the best customer is for your particular business at this exact moment in time!

Case Study: Sunbird Creative

When we first started Sunbird Creative, my business partner Mara and I thought we knew who our customers would be. Our strategy was simple and foolproof: We were going to work with local women business owners.

We lived in Harlem, a vibrant "village" we both adored. Best known for the Harlem Renaissance, the neighborhood has proudly held on to a unique identity throughout many decades of change. But rising living costs meant downtowners were arriving in unprecedented numbers, along with big box stores. We wanted to use our creative skills to help local businesses thrive in this newest wave of change. And because we were ourselves women entrepreneurs, we specifically wanted to serve other women.

After working remotely with clients from Texas to Korea, we thought our focus was extremely targeted. In honing in on target customers who fit all three demographics—being female, owning a business, and living in Harlem—we believed we had already identified our niche. All we needed to do as far as sales and marketing was to meet more people in this niche and do our thing.

Our first client was a local entrepreneur in her 70s. We had landed the ideal client!—or so we thought. It quickly became clear that something wasn't working. The small project spiraled out of control. Communication became difficult. Every conversation revealed unmet expectations on both sides. We were more excited to finish the project than we had been to start it. What had gone wrong?

Our first client met our initial criteria, but we weren't a good match. Over the next year, after working on dozens of projects, we realized that our ideal customer was a bit different than we initially thought. We paused to analyze which projects were the best and which were the worst. The patterns we found surprised us.

The first pattern we noticed was that the clients who got the most out of our services were tech-savvy—but not too tech-savvy. For many of our services, we used software that we found easy to use and easy to hand off to small business owners, such as Mailchimp and Squarespace. To get the most out of our work together, clients needed to be tech-savvy enough to learn and use these applications quickly. At the same time, entrepreneurs with more complex technological requirements would find our software too limiting.

How our clients used technology before working with us was a behavior that affected how valuable our services were to them and how efficiently we could provide them. Our first client wasn't used to the kinds of software we were used to. To her, they weren't "easy to use" at all! So we started looking for business owners who were already using certain kinds of software in their business. This behavior became more important in deciding whether or not a business owner was a good fit than whether they lived in the neighborhood or beyond it. We naturally found ourselves working with customers in other boroughs, as well as Long Island, Chicago, and DC.

While Mara and I started out with the assumption that we'd

naturally work well with all women entrepreneurs, we found that we actually worked very well with some men (gasp!) and terribly with some women. What made the difference? It largely came down to personality. We worked well with business owners who were a bit more sensitive and passion-driven than average, whether male or female. We struggled to connect with those on the opposite end of the spectrum.

While we had naturally focused on targeting customers according to their demographics, we realized that behaviors (like the use of technology) and psychographics (like personality) were much more important in finding the right customers for our brand.

Personality fit doesn't get talked about much in business, but it's a huge factor in face-to-face service businesses. Our first client was a no-nonsense serial entrepreneur who had fought to succeed in a world that privileged being male and being young. While we had a lot of respect for her and ultimately got the job done, we struggled to communicate every step of the way.

Honing in on our target customer was a great relief. We enjoy working with a variety of people, but dealing with less-than-ideal clients on less-than-ideal projects was less-than-enjoyable. It was also bad business. Spending tons of time putting out fires and managing expectations was inefficient and ultimately unprofitable. Just dealing with the consequences of targeting the wrong customers ate up time we could have spent on the actual work of branding.

Honing in on our target customer was also terrifying. Were there really enough sensitive, passion-driven business owners in our neighborhood with just the right level of tech-savviness to sustain our business? Unfortunately, the answer was no.

After looking at the data, we had to revise our niche. While we still adore Harlem and prioritize local clients, we are realistic about our strengths and limitations. There are simply some people we serve better than others, and those same people happen to appreciate our services more.

Redefining our target customer was a scary but exciting process that led to better branding and a more sustainable business model. It freed Mara and I to focus on activities we find both profitable and enjoyable—such as teaching, writing, and providing holistic branding services to businesses we believe in.

Why Your "Who" Matters

In talking to passionate small business owners about their brands, I used to begin with questions about their vision and mission—their Why. Our original process began with questions like, "If your brand could achieve its wildest dreams within 25 years, what would that look like?" and "Why do you do what you do?"

Our clients loved answering these questions, and I loved hearing their responses. It's magical to watch people reconnect with their passion and take the time, after months or years of getting lost in the weeds of logistics and administrative burdens, to tap into their vision. It was energizing. It was fun. And it was a mistake.

Don't get me wrong--I'm a big believer in the importance of tapping into your story and envisioning the future. When I feel lost, I journal about the past and then set 10-year goals, reminding myself where I come from and where I'm going. Taking ownership of your story and clarifying your values is extremely powerful and essential to an authentic brand. But it's not the right place to start.

After two years of starting our branding process off with these amazing conversations about the vision and mission of our clients, we realized we were experiencing an unintended side effect. The process was deeply affirming and encouraging, but this encouragement came at a cost. By focusing on the Why first, we were implying that the customer was secondary. We inadvertently sent the message that it was all right to ignore them.

You don't have to choose between your happiness and your customer's satisfaction. Not at all. You also don't have to buy in to the "customer is king" idea—and if you've had any time in business at all, you already know that the customer is not always right.

Your Why is the most personal part of your brand identity, and it's essential to both your motivation and your business' long-term success. Like any good leader, every business owner needs to be in tune with their Why. You need to understand where you're coming from, what you care about, and what your mission is to get other people on board with your ideas.

But here's the catch: The best leader is not really a leader without people willing to follow. In the same way, the best business owner is not really a business owner without customers.

When all is said and done, your brand exists because of your customers. Outside of a relationship with other people, it's just an idea in your head. The only way for any enterprise (businesses, nonprofits, even personal brands) to succeed is to provide value to real humans.

If I could only give one message to entrepreneurs everywhere, I would say this: Empathy matters as much as passion and vision. Without empathy, the strongest passion will blaze and burn out like a firecracker. Without empathy, vision will take you on a thrilling journey to nowhere. Why? Because caring about your customer is a prerequisite for every brand's goals: getting their attention, earning their trust, developing a thriving relationship.

Marketing guru Seth Godin puts it this way in his TED talk "Where Do Ideas Come From?":

> Consumers—and I don't just mean people who buy stuff at the Safeway, I mean people at the Defense Department who might buy something, people at the New Yorker who might print your article—consumers don't care about you at all. They just don't care. Part of the reason is that they've got way more choices than they used to and way less time. And in a world where we have too many choices and too little time, the obvious thing to do is just to ignore stuff.

Too many fresh entrepreneurs operate with a "build it and they will come" mentality. They believe their job is to craft the product of their dreams, and then let it free into a world of seven billion super-fans. Because what crazy person wouldn't buy the perfect product?

This attitude is very similar to the stereotypical proud parent. Never mind that their 30-year-old baby boy lives in their basement and has been playing Fortnite (without taking a shower) for the last two weeks straight... "Any girl would be lucky to have him!"

Both the dating world and the business world can be cutthroat—not because people are cruel but because their resources are limited. Everyone's got "too many choices and too little time." It's simply not possible for you to personally care for every one of the 7+ billion other people on the planet. And it's not possible for each of those 7+ billion people to personally care about you.

The challenge of marketing is often seen as getting as many people to care about you (and your brand) as possible. More customers = more success, right? But that's the wrong way to think about marketing, especially in the 21st century. In the mid-1900s, when TV, radio, and other one-way channels dominated, reach and exposure were everything. The companies with the biggest budgets got the most ads, and the companies with the most ads sold the most products. Consumers were used to one-way conversations. They watched the same shows as everyone else and read the same newspapers. They trusted big brands and commercials. Not anymore.

Targeting is becoming more and more possible, popular, and even expected. Inundated with a huge amount of information and advertising each day, most people don't want to hear about things that don't concern them. If you want their attention, you must make their importance to you and your value to them clear from the first impression. You can only do that when you know who you're talking to.

I promise you will save yourself a lot of time and trouble if you identify the kind of person most likely to buy your product or service, and sell directly to them. Why worry about the people your brand is not perfect for? Instead, look for the people who will not only buy from you but who will fall in love with your brand. Your business will be stronger for it.

Demographics

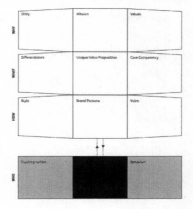

Demographics are the kind of data about your target customer you might find in a census, including:

- Age
- Gender
- Ethnicity
- Location
- Education
- Job
- Marital status
- Income

Some of these traits will be absolutely essential to your target customers. Others may be irrelevant. For example, where a target customer lives should be very important to a local dry cleaner, but may be trivial to an online coach. Naming gender may be essential to a fashion business, but unhelpful to a marriage therapist. Your goal is to capture the details that are important to your unique brand.

Defining demographics doesn't need to be a passive, check-the-box exercise. It can be both surprising and strategic. If you keep an open mind when defining demographics, you'll see that the lines between relevance and irrelevance are not always clear or obvious.

Look for interesting patterns among your past (or best) customers. If you're attentive, you might find that your customers have something in common that you would never have noticed. You might find that the people you thought you were speaking to aren't interested, but people you never thought to target are deeply attracted to your brand. Or you might see an opportunity to create a niche simply by targeting a more specific demographic than you've been targeting.

Example Demographics

- Small business owner
- 30-50 years old
- College educated
- Live in a large city
- Household income $80k+

Exercises

1. Have you tried targeting specific customers in the past? If yes, how did it go? If no, why not?
2. What demographics do your customers generally need to have to engage with your product or service? (For example, customers of a local business need to live in the neighborhood.)
3. Which of the following factors significantly affect how someone might interact with your brand?
   - Age
   - Gender
   - Employment
   - Education
   - Household Income
   - Personal Income

- o   Location
- o   Race or Ethnicity

4. Collect all your customer data in a table. Do you see any patterns in terms of demographic characteristics?

5. Identify your favorite or best customers from the table you've just created. Do you see any patterns in terms of demographic characteristics?

Psychographics

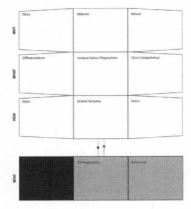

Psychographics describe how your target customer thinks and feels, including:

- Attitudes
- Beliefs
- Tastes
- Desires
- Personality traits

Psychographic data include details we tend to associate with being unique individuals. They're the subjective details that spark compassion and insight—they bring your customer alive. Knowing that your spa's target customers are women is good; knowing whether they're women who believe that spa treatments are fun indulgences or women who believe treatments have the power to heal mind, body, and soul is better.

Just as with demographics, you're looking for meaningful patterns in the psychographics of your target customers. And just as with demographics, some of those patterns may be obvious, but many are not. There is nothing more powerful in marketing than understanding your target customer, and psychographics provide the deepest form of understanding.

While target customer demographics are telling, psychographics can explain a lot of the variation between brands in the same industry. Consider Walmart, Target, and Bloomingdales. In the broad universe of business types, they are practically identical. Yet you probably have very different associations with each of them. Why is that?

The fact that they target slightly different demographics—especially when it comes to income and age—is one obvious answer. But the genius (and ongoing challenge) of these brands is in understanding the hearts and minds of their customers. As a Millennial woman living in close proximity to all three of these stores, I have very specific reasons for choosing among them that have very little to do with the products they sell and a lot more to do with the messaging they put out and the experience they create. I go to Walmart when I want to be thrifty, Target when I want retail therapy, and Bloomingdales when I want to feel like an adult.

When Mara and I realized that our customers no longer fit the demographic mold we had created (women solopreneurs of any age), it would have been tempting to simply widen our net. It's very easy to expand your target customer to fit every exception to the rule... until your "target" is so vague you don't know what you're aiming for anymore. But while it's almost always better to err on the side of specificity, it's possible to be arbitrarily rigid in defining your niche.

As we looked at our customers, we realized that we were attracting men as well as women (less specific than we thought), small business owners as well as solopreneurs (less specific than we thought), and far more Gen Xers than those of any other age group (more specific than we thought). What was going on?

We discovered that many of our best customers had very specific psychographics in common. They shared certain attitudes toward business, technology, and even themselves that made our specific way of working extremely valuable and refreshing. And because providing face-to-face services is a very intimate interaction, personality fit also played a big role. As it turned out, it mattered more whether a potential customer was sensitive and creative than whether they were male or female.

These kinds of realizations free you to serve humans who will fall in love with your brand, rather than spend time chasing down others who might buy from you once but never become a fan. It may feel awkward at first to name specific psychographics of your target customer, but nothing will set you up better for branding strategically and marketing effectively.

Example Psychographics

- Sensitive and resourceful personalities
- Believe that business should be profitable and do good
- Tend to think outside the box but don't consider themselves creatives or innovators
- Passionate about their work but highly value work/life balance

Exercises

1. What kind of people has your brand naturally attracted, even without much effort?
2. What kind of people are not attracted to your brand? Why not?
3. Think of your least favorite customer. Who were they and what made them your least favorite?
4. Imagine your ideal customer—someone who would become a repeat customer and loyal fan, someone who would tell all their friends about your business. Give them a name and describe them.
5. Using the list of best or favorite customers from the demographics exercises, note any patterns you find in terms of the following:
   o Personalities

- o Beliefs
- o Interests
- o Hobbies
- o Desires
- o Values
- o Lifestyles

Behaviors

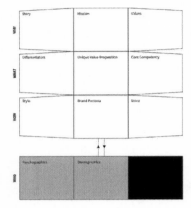

Behaviors describe actions your target customers take that are relevant to your brand, which may include:

- How they try to solve the problem your business solves
- How they compare and evaluate before a purchase
- How they tend to buy similar products or services
- How they consume information (and what forms of media they consume)
- How they spend their free time

Marketers often lump behaviors under "psychographics," but in my experience it's much easier and more productive to distinguish between the two. To return to the spa example, women who see spa treatments as fun indulgences (psychographic) may have a very different path to actually purchasing them (behavior). One woman may only visit spas sporadically with friends and rely exclusively on word-of-mouth recommendations, while another woman makes monthly solo appointments at whatever place happens to be offering the best deal. You can start to see how a spa's brand may differ according to the behaviors of their target customer.

While thinking through behaviors is the most practical part of defining your Who, it can also lead to profound insights. It's your chance to think through a day in the life of your target customer. How are they currently addressing the need you want to fill? How do their values and lifestyle translate into actions and habits?

When you're thinking about your customer's behaviors, it's extremely important to note whether they match your small business' limitations and strengths. When you find a mismatch, you can choose to adjust your target customer or adjust your business. Either way, you'll be better able to understand and serve the humans to whom your brand is dedicated.

When Mara and I noticed that we worked best with entrepreneurs in their 30s and 40s, we realized it was largely because of their behavioral tendencies. In our experience, compared with other age groups, Gen X entrepreneurs tend to enjoy learning new technologies but aren't totally comfortable with them. They want to do as much as they can on their own but are willing to outsource specific projects when they find someone trustworthy.

Because Sunbird Creative's services are project-based and involve easy-to-use software, we are a perfect fit for entrepreneurs with these behaviors. By the same token, our business is not a good match for entrepreneurs who, wanting to be as hands-off as possible, outsource freely to specialists and are used to the features of expensive software.

Just as with demographics and psychographics, seeing these meaningful patterns in the behavior of our target customer has helped us be much more efficient in our marketing and effective in our services. It's liberating to stop pursuing the people who aren't a good match for your business and focus on serving the people you're best at serving. That attitude makes for a much stronger brand and a much more sustainable business.

Example Behaviors

- Try to do most business functions on their own at first but will eventually outsource
- Rely on easy-to-use software
- Hire one-off rather than ongoing services
- Join local small business groups for support

Exercises

1. How do your customers find out about your brand?
2. What do your customers do before deciding to buy from you? (For example: read reviews, call, compare prices, check your social media, etc.)
3. What skills or habits do your customers need to already have in order to engage with your brand? (For example: use a computer, visit farmer's markets, attend industry conferences, etc.)
4. Using the list of favorite or best customers from previous exercises, can you think of any behaviors they have in common?
5. Think of your ideal customer again. Write out a schedule of everything they might do, hour by hour, throughout a normal day.

Key Takeaways

- The Who in your Brand Canvas answers the question, "Who will fall in love with your brand?"
- The type of person who is most likely to fall in love with your brand is your target customer. A target customer description should be less specific than an "individual customer profile" and more specific than a "target market." The sweet spot in between is where you have enough detail to connect meaningfully with the group of people who fit that description but not so much detail that the group is only comprised of five individuals.
- It's important to understand three key aspects of your target customer: their psychographics (what they think, feel, and believe), demographics (the kind of information you'd find in a census), and behaviors (what they do).
- Your goal is to identify traits that most of your best customers have in common, so that you can find and speak to more humans just like them. Thinking outside the box and looking for surprising patterns in the data is often key to creating a strong target customer description.
- By keeping your target customer at the forefront of your mind, you'll prevent the majority of branding headaches and more quickly resolve the toughest branding challenges.
- The days of reaching the "average" person through mass media channels are over. This is great news for small business owners who are willing to embrace the discipline of speaking directly to target customers and developing a niche.

WHY

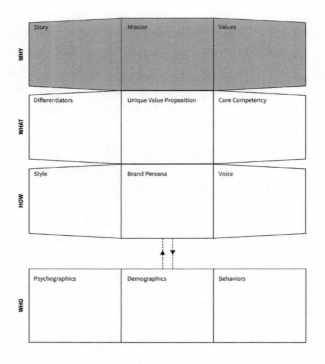

Why does your business exist?

Your "Why" taps into the deepest part of your brand. It is the juice, the mojo of your brand. It's the motivation behind all your activities, the passion that drives the organization forward. It's what gets your brand out of bed in the morning. And it contains three overlapping elements:

- Story
- Mission
- Values

Your Why is more likely to be at the back of your mind than at the forefront of your marketing. A business' Why has a direct impact on whether you and your team feel inspired to do great work, and an indirect impact on whether your target customer decides to do business with you.

But make no mistake: Customers care about your story, mission, and values. Articulating your Why clearly will help you stay motivated and focused. It will also help you figure out how to connect on a deeper level with your target customers.

Case Study: Becoming Better Together

After two years of successfully working together on myriad projects, the team behind the coaching collaborative BBT was ready to build a unified brand. But they faced a unique challenge: How would they build a streamlined, coherent brand based on a team of six diverse women (plus one man) with different backgrounds (in HR, non-profits, academia, and professional coaching) who provided over a dozen services (from data evaluation to retreats)?

It was clear from the moment we met BBT that their Why anchored their brand and would become a cornerstone for all of our future branding decisions. The clues were there in our first interaction: Their full name, "Becoming Better Together," puts inclusiveness and collaboration at the forefront of their identity. In their first email to us, explaining what they were looking for in creative partners, they wrote: "We felt a strong kinship with what you share and how you work." This was clearly a company steeped in a set of strong values.

As we got to know the women behind BBT, our intuitions were confirmed. An ambitious shared mission—to solve the biggest cultural problems of large organizations—fueled them. But their story, mission, and values weren't just the glue that held them together behind the scenes. Their Why turned out to be the cornerstone of their brand, the key to both their credibility and differentiation.

In the world of organizational and professional development, terms like "Diversity, Equity, and Inclusiveness" are trendy. But few consulting firms truly understand DEI—and even fewer actually practice those principles in their own organizations. BBT's excellent track record, collaborative approach, and diverse team put them in a position to overtake more established coaching and consulting brands when it came to building more diverse and inclusive organizational cultures.

Many brands do not explicitly feature their Why at the forefront of their brand, although strong brands allow their Why to infuse every aspect of their business. (Consider the connection between Nike or Apple's taglines, mission statements, and products.) Because of the nature of their work, BBT's Why mattered more to their target customers than usual. We didn't ignore their Who, What, or How in order to focus on their Why. In fact, our biggest challenges were a) to use jargon-free language about their mission that their target customers could easily relate to, and b) capture their bold but grounded personality in visuals that appealed to executives.

Expressing your mission in words and images that are meaningful to you is a great starting point, but a good branding process will shape those expressions into something that resonates profoundly with other humans—your target customers.

Why Your "Why" Matters

Big brands have been losing a lot of trust in the last few decades, as we become more skeptical as consumers and citizens. We've gotten used to having too much information, sifting through tons of options, and being lied to by corporations and politicians.

That's great news for small brands. Why? Because being authentic—telling the truth, sharing your story, and sticking to your values—is at a premium. Multiple studies confirm that consumers, especially in the younger generations, are willing to pay more for brands that share their values:

- In 2015, a Nielson study that spanned 60 countries found that 66% of all respondents and 73% of Millennials are willing to pay more for sustainable consumer goods.[1]
- In 2017, a Cone Communications study found that 87% of American consumers say they would do business with a brand just because it advocated for an issue they cared about.[2]
- In 2018, a DoSomething Strategic study found that 89% of Gen Z consumers have boycotted or would consider boycotting a brand that doesn't align with their values.[3]

Consumer activism is on the rise. More and more, people expect brands to share their motives and beliefs if they want to earn their trust. I believe that the days are gone in which the average person was okay with the idea that the purpose of a business is simply to make a profit.

But no matter how eager you are to do good, you are still a

---

[1] https://www.nielsen.com/us/en/press-room/2015/consumer-goods-brands-that-demonstrate-commitment-to-sustainability-outperform.html
[2] https://sustainablebrands.com/read/marketing-and-comms/new-report-reveals-86-of-us-consumers-expect-companies-to-act-on-social-environmental-issues
[3] https://sustainablebrands.com/read/walking-the-talk/brands-take-note-gen-z-is-putting-its-money-where-its-values-are

business owner, not a nonprofit executive. You know that you need to keep an eye on the bottom line or risk going under. So where does profit fit into the equation?

The most brilliant and useful way to think about profit I've ever heard comes from Jim Collins' book Good to Great. After carefully studying 11 publicly-traded companies that wildly out-performed both the stock market and very similar competitors for at least a decade, Collins finds that these companies consistently (among other things) stuck to a few core values—even when it hurt. Sticking to these values sometimes came at a financial cost, yet in the end these companies outperformed the stock market by a factor of at least three.

After spending decades delving into the differentiators of great companies, Collins summarizes the perspective of these amazing organizations in a profound metaphor:

"Profit is like the health of a business."

When you're in very poor health, it's hard to do or think about anything beyond taking care of yourself. Whenever I get the flu, my world gets very small. My ambitions are reduced to one thing: being healthy again. But my life is not normally about avoiding the flu. Few people are so obsessed with wellness that they try to stay healthy for the sake of... health. While there's certainly pleasure in not being sick (I often find myself on a high for days after overcoming the flu, for example, until good health becomes normal again), most of us take care of ourselves so that we can do things other than take of ourselves.

Getting a good night's sleep enables me to show up to work with fresh ideas for our clients instead of mechanically going through the motions. Eating throughout the day enables me to spend an evening enjoying a pleasant conversation with my husband rather than expressing whatever 'hangry' thoughts happen to cross my mind. Exercising regularly gives me the strength to trek through the city to visit friends, climb the stairs to church, shop for a whole week's groceries, and do a ton of other meaningful activities without injuring or exhausting myself.

If your business is not profitable, please take care of it. Like newborn babies, new brands often suck a lot more from you than they can give back. It's up to you how long you'll tolerate this imbalance for; there are different theories on how long a business can be unprofitable before it's deemed unhealthy or defunct.

Just keep in mind that all healthy businesses are profitable, but not all profitable businesses are successful. A successful business is profitable without losing its soul. Profit helps you achieve your Why without being your Why.

Your business does not exist solely to make a profit. So why does it exist?

If you can tell your brand story with passion, articulate your mission with conviction, and name your values with sincerity, your brand will be able to tap into the some of the deepest parts of the human psyche. More than the latest win or next opportunity, your Why will motivate you and your team to do good work and keep going. And more than a cool feature or clever tagline, your Why will connect you with target customers on an emotional level.

Your Why is what makes your brand authentic and meaningful. It's what makes your marketing more than a gimmick and your business more than a profit-producing machine. It's what inspires your target customers to trust you.

Story

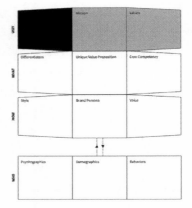

Story is hot these days. The prominence of digital marketing—which takes social media and video very seriously—has catapulted "storytelling" to the front of every marketer's mind. But as Pamela B. Rutledge, PhD, MBA, writes in her article in Psychology Today, "There have been stories and messages delivered across different media ever since the Cro-Magnon man figured out that mineral pigments like iron oxide and black manganese could be applied to the sides of rocks and caves."[4]

Humans are hard-wired for stories. As someone who's a lot better at talking about words and ideas than people and plots, I used to think that storytelling was optional. I believed that some people had the gift of story. These are the people who can magically captivate you with impersonations and unexpected twists, who can take an ordinary experience and turn it into a hilarious adventure or inspiring journey. The rest of us, I believed, were fated to be a passive audience, enjoying the stories we're told, but unable to make them ourselves.

---

[4] https://www.psychologytoday.com/us/blog/positively-media/201101/the-psychological-power-storytelling

Psychology has proven me wrong time and time again. While it may be true that telling interesting stories comes more naturally to some, we are all telling stories all the time. There are no exceptions. It's how we make meaning out of our experiences. It's not optional, and it's not occasional. We don't just engage with stories when we go to the movies or read news articles and novels. We wake up in a story of who we are, as characters in a plot, and we live that drama out from morning to night, over and over again. What's a "good" or "bad" day but a description of how our plot is working out? Even as we sleep, our brains are turning our disjointed thoughts, emotions, and sensations into dreams. We literally can't stop putting the pieces of our experience into a meaningful order.

Stories are how we make sense of ourselves, other people, and the world at large. They're a shortcut to empathy and deep understanding. That's why stories are much more effective tools for persuasion (and sales) than dry facts. What are you more likely to remember about a presidential candidate: details of their tax reform proposal or details about the time they spent in their family's hardware store as a child?

The same principle that applies to personal brands and personal relationships applies to your business: Telling stories helps you make an emotional connection and develop trust.

So how do you figure out your brand's story? In business, it's usually better to make your target customer the protagonist in your storytelling. Nothing convinces a person you know how to help them quicker than telling them their own story—including, of course, how your brand fits in. That being said, telling your own story (and how your customer fits in) is an important part of developing a brand that feels authentic and trustworthy. Your story is often the vehicle for communicating your values and mission. Because, once again, it's a lot easier to understand and remember a story than a list of bullet points or an abstract statement.

Therefore the goal of the Story section in your Brand Canvas is not to tell your customer's story but your own. Think of it as your brand's origin story. While your customer is the hero of the drama, what we're trying to capture is the backstory of their sidekick, your brand.

Of course, there's not one right way to tell your story. But here are a few principles to keep in mind:

Every story contains two main components: a protagonist (with a personality, goals, and desires), and a plot (made up of events organized into beginning, middle, and end).

The easiest way to think about your brand story is as an answer to the question: "Why does your business exist?"

Many businesses leave out the human protagonist from their story with vague language like "Since 1985, Company X has been making widgets for people…" This is a missed opportunity to make a true emotional connection, especially for small businesses. Don't worry about making your brand sound bigger, older, or more professional than it actually is. Your main goal is not to write a resume for a judgmental employer but to connect emotionally with people who want to understand where you're coming from.

Telling a true story is more about what you don't say than about what you do say. The unedited version of why and how you started your business could probably span several books. Your challenge is to turn that messy reality into a memorable, easy-to-follow plot.

Know what's at stake. A story with nothing at stake is not an interesting one. The plot is exciting when the protagonist is seeking or fighting for something that matters.

While your customer isn't the protagonist of your brand story, keep in mind that they are your audience. Include the details that matter to them. Does the fact that you started your local business in another state before moving it to your current city make it more or less credible to your target customer? Does the fact that you tested your product on your own child make you more or less relatable? There are no hard-and-fast answers to these kinds of questions, because different target customers may have different responses to the same information. Find a way to tell your story that resonates.

Your brand story is not a single set of plot points set in stone. Practice telling your story in slightly different ways and see what resonates. And remember that your story will evolve as your business evolves.

You have just enough space in your Brand Canvas to name the protagonist and most basic outline of your story's plot. This is intentional. Remember that this shortened version of your story is not for your target customer's eyes. You'll expand on it later. What's most important now is that you capture the essential elements in their simplest form.

Example Story

A freelance designer and copywriter in Harlem partner up to serve local businesses. They realize that a weak brand is at the core of many clients' marketing struggles, so they develop a simple but effective branding methodology for small business.

Exercises

1. Why did you start your company?
2. How (and with whom) did you start your company?
3. What have been your biggest milestones?
4. What have been your biggest challenges?
5. Write your story in three sections: beginning, middle, and end. Now summarize each section in one sentence.
6. Look at your story in the eyes of your target customer. What do they find most interesting?
7. If a newspaper ran an article about your brand story, how would the headline read?

Mission

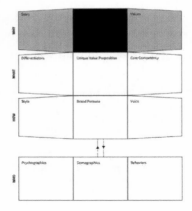

The core of your brand's "Why" is your Mission. Mission describes the reason your business does what it does. Your story describes the way you arrived at this mission. Your values describe the way you intend to carry it out.

A strong mission lifts your business out of the realm of pure economics and helps your brand connect deeply with your target market. It also gives you a laser-like focus when it comes to making business decisions by defining what success means to you.

If you have any experience in a corporate or nonprofit setting, you likely have strong opinions of the phrase "mission statement." You may associate it with meandering meetings, half-hearted attempts at employee engagement, shady corporate and social responsibility campaigns—in short, BS. Or you may have experienced the unstoppable energy of a diverse team united around a single goal.

If you're a skeptic of the value of mission statements, consider that people are by nature goal-oriented. We are so goal-oriented, in fact, that there's a theory within cognitive science that basically states that our brains don't perceive objects; we perceive tools. Everything we do is for an end. We live off goals. The future feeds us. Just think of the last time you achieved a difficult ambition. Were you content to sit back, rest on your laurels, and enjoy your success for the rest of your life? Or did you move on quickly to the next challenge?

Mission statements are incredibly useful tools because we are goal-oriented creatures. A solid mission statement will help you (and your team) stay laser-focused and hyper-motivated.

If you're a detail-oriented doer, the kind of person who can get lost in the weeds, a mission statement serves as your north star. It will remind you of the bigger picture on the days you're overwhelmed by the day-to-day.

If you're a big-picture thinker, the kind of person who easily floats off into space, a mission statement serves as your anchor. It will remind you of what matters most on the days you're tempted to start a hundred new projects you'll probably never finish.

A good mission statement serves as a litmus test for new opportunities. It will help you make good choices and avoid distractions. Businesses that aren't clear about their mission are at risk of spreading themselves too thin, confusing their customers, and diluting their brand. Business owners with a clear mission can tell whether a new opportunity (such as a potential partnership or project) is worth exploring just by answering the question: "Does this serve or distract from our mission?"

Your mission defines success for your business in the bigger picture. When you don't meet a short-term goal, it can be hard to know whether your business is on the right track overall. Having a clear mission helps you track the metric that matters most to you. If you didn't meet your monthly revenue goal but did delight your customers or protect the environment (for example), you can still feel good about what you accomplished. On the other hand, if you exceeded your revenue goal but made your customers' lives more difficult or hurt the environment, you might need to reassess your priorities.

When they're genuine, mission statements are incredibly motivating. If you're working alone, it will be the voice that reminds you why you started on this journey. If you're working with a partner or a team, it will be your rallying cry. When people are really committed to a mission, even the most mundane tasks become imbued with purpose and meaning. As humans, we need more than a paycheck or a pat on the back to feel engaged in our work.

In addition to helping you stay focused and motivated behind the scenes, a mission statement helps your target customers understand why your business exists. Without a clear purpose beyond making money, businesses can seem heartless and greedy. Articulating your motives for engaging in revenue-generating activities helps customers understand and trust your brand.

You don't need to be a social enterprise to have an inspiring Mission. Social enterprises hold themselves accountable to a high bar when it comes to purpose. They're more likely to publicize their mission and incorporate it into their branding and marketing. In other words, they spend more time than average thinking about Mission. Whether or not you describe your business as a social enterprise, you can think clearly and strategically about your mission too.

If you're honest about your motives and careful about choosing your target customers, your mission will resonate with them. Whether or not they're already passionate about your cause, they'll probably agree that your mission is good and worth pursuing.

Great mission statements help customers feel like they're part of something bigger than a monetary transaction when they engage with your business. They generate a kind of enthusiasm that no product or personality could create on its own. There's nothing quite like getting together with like-minded people to serve a bigger purpose.

Because your mission should help you make business decisions and be relevant to your target customers, it's important to be strategic in how you describe it. There are likely several personal and practical reasons behind why you started your business. You don't have to capture all of them in your mission to be authentic. In fact, it's very important (and very difficult!) to be specific and clear. Whatever your reasons for starting the business were, consider what's keeping it alive now. If your business closed down tomorrow, the world would be a little worse off. Why?

There are many different philosophies on how long a mission statement should be. For the purpose of your Brand Profile, err on the side of short and sweet. A good rule of thumb is to keep it concise enough that it's easy to remember and specific enough that it's worth remembering.

Example Mission

To help underserved, socially conscious small businesses become more sustainable by developing a brand identity that's unique, authentic, and attractive to a niche market.

Exercises

1. What problems do you most like to solve for customers?
2. What do you believe makes a business great?
3. What drives you to continue in your work, even when things are hard?
4. What causes or movements do you want your business to be part of?
5. What's the biggest thing you can imagine achieving with your brand in 25 years?
6. Looking back, how will you know if your business was successful?
7. If you're stuck or need a starting point, try out these templates:
   o Our mission is to help [target customer] do [activity].

o Our mission is to solve [problem] by [specific action].

o Our mission is to [goal] by [how to achieve goal].

o Our mission is to contribute to [value or cause] by creating [product/service type] that [function or differentiator].

Values

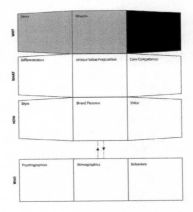

If your business were a person, how would it decide what's right and wrong? What would its guiding principles be? Would it care more about efficiency or inner peace?

While your story hints at what matters to your business, a list of values lays it out explicitly. Values are like guideposts to help you make strategic decisions, build a company culture you love (even if you're a one-person business), and find target customers who naturally care about your brand. Clear values can help you find like-minded suppliers and partners, recruit and train ideal employees, and give you insights about your target customers.

Patagonia, an American outdoor clothing company, is a great example of clear core values. Theirs elaborate on exactly how they intend to fulfill their planet-saving mission: "build the best product," "cause no unnecessary harm," "use business to protect nature," and "not bound by convention." (As a writer, I'm a bit annoyed at the lack of parallelism of the last value, which is just a passive description rather than an active verb phrase, but the editorial oversight hasn't affected their success.)

These phrases, which Patagonia elaborates on in their website, reflect a very specific point of view on business and society. The company has a clear perspective both on what's wrong with the world and how to fix it. These values guide how they source and design their products. They also attract people who are more likely to pay a higher price and become loyal fans than people who are just looking for the lowest price on a fleece sweater.

If you've never explicitly named values either in your personal or professional life before, the task can seem overwhelming. Many people come out of their first values exercise with a very vague set of words. I think this happens because it can feel wrong to elevate some values over others. What does it mean about you if your business cares more about innovation than environmental responsibility? Does valuing beauty or status make you a superficial person?

It takes courage to look your brand in the face, warts and all, because it is a reflection of you to some degree. How you run your business does say something about you as a person. That's part of what makes it meaningful. Embrace this opportunity to learn something about yourself and stand by what matters to you. No one in the world has exactly the same set of values you do. That means you won't build a brand that gets everyone's approval. What matters is that you're honest with yourself and find customers who care about some of the same things you care about.

Another helpful way to approach values is as an exercise in prioritization. Rather than think about choosing between values that are diametrically opposed (like form vs. function, or results vs. work-life balance), think about building a hierarchy of values. In this frame of mind, you aren't rejecting values; you're simply stacking them relative to one another. Your goal is to figure out what values belong at the top of your hierarchy, so that you can focus your limited mindspace and resources on that part of the pyramid.

Naming your values is a way to hold your business accountable to what matters—to you and to your customers. Your customers care about issues and expect you to care too. In 2018, an Edelman Earned Brand study found that 64% of consumers around the world will buy or boycott a brand exclusively because of where it stands on a social or political issue.[5]

You will never meet everyone's ethical standards all the time. But you can consistently meet the ones that are most important—if you name them. Be proactive. Don't let your business slip into trendy or conventional practices. Seize the opportunity to make your business and your brand even more meaningful.

So how do you go about naming your values? What language do you use? Once again, there is no right way. Here are a few tips I've found most helpful after helping dozens of small business owners and looking at hundreds of examples:

Be honest. Your values should represent what you actually care about as a business, not what you wish you cared about or plan to care about in the future. There's a place for aspirational values in your planning and strategy, but for the sake of your brand do not hold yourself to unattainable standards. Failing to live out an aspirational value you want to be known for is not a good alternative to naming values you already easily live out.

While you can try to capture each value in a single word (such as "transparency"), every word has so many connotations that it can seem pretty meaningless. If you happen to have a very specific definition of a single-word value in mind, feel free to use it in your Brand Canvas—just be sure to elaborate on it elsewhere.

Stating your values as imperatives (i.e. commands) can make them much more personal and dynamic. For example, Patagonia's "cause no unnecessary harm" is a lot more evocative and specific than the phrase "avoiding harm" or the word "harmlessness."

Please don't use the word integrity. Integrity describes someone who sticks to their values. "Integrity" is not a value in itself, just as

---

[5] https://www.edelman.com/news-awards/two-thirds-consumers-worldwide-now-buy-beliefs

"colorful" is not a color.

Aim for 3-5 values. Any more becomes hard to remember and even harder to implement consistently. Feel free to elaborate on these in your internal materials, such as employee handbooks.

Example Values

- Respect every human, including yourself
- Encourage always and honestly
- Aim at what's good for both the business and the soul

Exercises

1. Think of two business owners you think highly of, whether you know them or have only heard of them. Which of their character traits do you respect?
2. What values do you expect the businesses you deal with to uphold?
3. You'd rather fail (and let your brand fail) than become _____.
4. Imagine you're interviewing a potential new employee. You're going to work with this person on a daily basis, and they're going to interact with customers regularly. What three things do you want them to value?
5. Highlight three values from the following list that your brand most cares about. (These should be values that your team adheres to and that your business operates by.) Are there other phrases that come to mind?
    o   Achieving Excellence
    o   Achieving High Status
    o   Attaining Balance
    o   Being Transparent
    o   Bringing People Together

- o Changing the Status Quo
- o Connecting with Roots
- o Creating Joy
- o Developing Expertise
- o Developing Wealth
- o Energizing People
- o Evoking Pride
- o Growing Knowledge
- o Impacting Society
- o Increasing Efficiency
- o Inspiring Curiosity
- o Inspiring Exploration
- o Nurturing Faith
- o Providing Security
- o Provoking New Ideas
- o Seeking Justice
- o Taking Responsibility

Key Takeaways

- The Why in your Brand Canvas answers the question "Why does your brand exist?"
- At a time when brands have to work extra hard to earn trust, an authentic Why connects you with customers in a way that nothing else can.
- Even if you never put your mission, story, or values at the forefront of your marketing, being able to clearly articulate them has huge benefits to your business behind the scenes. They motivate you and your team, create a strong company culture, and help you focus on what's most important.
- Your brand story should feature a protagonist in pursuit of something that matters.
- Your values should honestly and specifically reflect what matters most to your business.
- Your mission is the anchor of your Why. If your business were a person, it would be their calling in life.

WHAT

WHY	Story	Mission	Values
WHAT	Differentiators	Unique Value Proposition	Core Competency
HOW	Style	Brand Persona	Voice
WHO	Psychographics	Demographics	Behaviors

What are your superpowers?

Every business has strengths and weaknesses. Human branding is not about covering up the weaknesses or making your business appear better than it is. It's about showing off what makes your brand attractive to your target customers.

Your "What" is comprised of three elements:

- Differentiators
- Unique Value Proposition
- Core Competency

In trying to compete with other brands on price or quality, many small businesses miss out on a chance to win the hearts of target customers. Communicating what your business is truly great at and what sets you apart from similar business helps the right humans fall in love with your brand faster.

Every small business has superpowers. The challenge for most business owners is getting specific about what they are.

Case Study: Massawa

Massawa is an Eritrean-Ethiopian restaurant in Upper Manhattan. The family-owned small business had been in operation for 30 years when Yohanes Tekeste, the founder's son, reached out to Mara and me. The restaurant was changing in big ways and needed a new brand to match exciting new developments: a total renovation and the launch of its first packaged product, a split pea shiro that customers adored.

Yohanes wanted to share Eritrean and Ethiopian cuisine with people who had never tried East African food—and especially the students, staff, and tourists who passed by every day. But competition was fierce, not only among lunch spots near Columbia University, but also among Ethiopian restaurants in NYC. Over the years, more than a dozen had cropped up in Manhattan alone.

Massawa had survived thirty years in NYC's cutthroat restaurant environment, consistently earning 4+ stars on every review platform. But Yohanes knew that taking advantage of their expansion to thrive would require a stronger, more strategic brand. Being another good Ethiopian restaurant simply wasn't good enough.

By deep-diving into reviews, customer testimonials, and interviews with Yohanes, we identified the differentiators that would set Massawa's updated business apart from the rest: its authenticity combined with its accessibility. Massawa is arguably NYC's oldest African eatery—run by the Millennial children of its first-generation founders. Yohanes' parents ensured that the food remained authentic and high-quality; he and his siblings would ensure that the experience appealed to younger customers unfamiliar with East African culture. That balanced combination of authenticity and accessibility translated to modernized decor, longer open hours, vegan-friendly options, an easy-to-navigate menu, and a minimalist look directly inspired by Eritrean art.

Anyone who believes in the inherent value of their product or service will be tempted to gloss over the all-important step of naming their brand's unique value proposition. Massawa was able to thrive for many years as "that really good Ethiopian restaurant in Upper Manhattan." But the moment competition creeps in or you want to reach new target customers, you need to know what makes your brand unique and valuable. This is the core of your brand. Massawa's What is their ability to blend authenticity and accessibility. What's yours?

Why Your "What" Matters

The What section of your Brand Canvas—your differentiators, unique value proposition, and core competency—is where brand strategy overlaps with business strategy. These aspects of your business aren't just good for your marketing. They're essential to any business that intends to survive, let alone thrive, in the long run.

Conventional business education tends to assume that business strategy is simple and linear: First you figure out what your product and its value proposition are (what you're selling and what gap it fills in the market); then you create a marketing plan (exactly how you'll provide that offering and to whom); then, as time allows, you worry about branding (sometimes thought of as adding personality or style to your marketing materials).

The reality, however, is usually much more complex. It's more realistic to think of business, product, marketing, and brand strategy as different perspectives on the same problem. Every decision you make within your business will affect your brand and vice versa.

For example, if you decide to manufacture in China purely for financial reasons, without paying any mind to "branding" as such, your customers' perception of your product will be different than if you manufactured in, say, the US. Whether your price point is high or low, what marketing channels you focus on, how you handle customer complaints, what operations processes you implement— these all have a direct effect on your brand. And the personality that comes through in the tone of your social media content, the look and language of your website, your packaging design, even your email signatures—these have a direct effect on your bottom line.

All this is to say that the lines between "business" and "brand" strategy are blurry. As I alluded to before, one useful way to think about it is to consider "branding" a lens through which you look at the business. When you put on your Brand Manager hat, you're looking at your business through the eyes of outsiders. How do the decisions made within your business appear to the rest of the world, especially your target customers?

When you put on your Business Manager hat, the decision of what accounting and invoicing software to use may involve questions like "Which is easiest for me and my team to use? What does it cost every month? What functionalities are must-haves vs. nice-to-haves? How does it integrate with our other software? Is our accountant familiar with it?"

At the same time, the Brand Manager inside you is looking at that same decision from the perspective of your customers, asking questions like, "What's it like for a customer to receive an invoice from this software? Can we customize the template with our logo and colors so clients know instantly who it's coming from?"

Of course, the Business Manager and Brand Manager inside you need to work together. If the Brand Manager chooses the sexiest accounting software available, but it happens to be the most expensive and difficult to use, both your brand and business will probably suffer.

Your What is the place where your Business Manager and Brand Manager need to be perfectly in sync. It matters perhaps more than any other aspect of your Brand Canvas because it can make or break a business. Your What can carry the rest of your brand. In fact, many small businesses thrive without ever giving much thought to brand personalities, mission statements, or target customers. How? By owning their unique value proposition and letting all their decisions flow naturally from it.

It's scary to think about your What if you expect, as a small business, to be "the best" in your class or industry. Forget it. Small businesses don't have the resources to be the best—not in a vague, general way. But you will be able to be the best at something—if you're willing to get really specific about what that something is. Sometimes what makes a brand great isn't even about being the best at all; sometimes it's about being funnier, or more caring, or simply refreshingly different.

It's important to compare your business to others so you understand what makes your brand better than others—in very specific ways, for very specific target customers. If you're willing to look honestly at the strengths and limitations of both your business and your competitors, you'll be able to build a very strong basis for your brand very quickly. You won't waste time pretending to be like another brand, and you won't waste time making vague and unsupported claims about your business. You'll communicate clearly, effectively, and confidently what sets your unique brand apart.

Wonder Woman doesn't waste time wishing she were Spiderman. Aquaman doesn't waste time learning how to fly. Batman doesn't worry about what people will think about his outfit.

When you're comfortable with your unique superpowers, you're focused on what's most important: fulfilling your mission—and having some fun along the way.

Differentiators

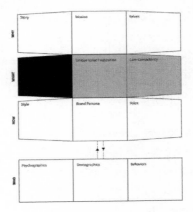

Differentiation is exactly what it sounds like: making sure your brand is different from competitors. Of course, no two businesses are exactly the same. So why bother thinking deeply about what makes yours different?

The goal of differentiation is to own and communicate the differences you want to be known for. Sometimes differentiating more effectively means emphasizing certain aspects of your brand that are already present (such as an innovative feature of your product). Sometimes it means making a decisive choice between two conflicting messages or personality traits (such as "We're bold and unapologetic" and "We're warm and comfortable"). And sometimes it means adding a component to your brand that was missing before (such as featuring the story behind the chef on a sauce label).

Differentiation is not about doing whatever it takes for the sake of standing out. This approach will get you eyeballs, but it won't get you hearts and minds. Unless your Brand Persona involves being loud and colorful, you can't differentiate just by turning up the volume. Aim instead at finding your tune and playing it consistently.

I've found that many entrepreneurs tend to fall into one of two traps when it comes to differentiating from their competitors: believing that their product or service alone differentiates their brand from competitors, or not taking their competitors seriously.

In the first case, entrepreneurs who are not used to accounting for the psychology of marketing believe that their differentiator is simply having "the best" product or service. This belief is full of (usually untested) assumptions. It assumes that business is not about a relationship but about a transaction—you give a stranger a product, then the stranger pays you exactly what it's worth. For better or for worse, there's a lot more to it than that. This attitude also assumes that being confident about the value you offer eliminates the need to consider your target customer's perspective and package it in a way that appeals to them.

The features of your offerings are important, but almost never as important as makers and entrepreneurs tend to think they are. The key to picking features to emphasize and communicating about them well is understanding what's important to your target customer. Does it matter to them that your salsa is "perfectly balanced"? It might, if they're middle-aged foodies on the hunt for perfection. It might not, if they're college freshmen on the hunt for cheap party snacks.

If you believe that having "the best" product or service is all you need, consider this: What on Earth does "best" even mean? Is there anything that the world unanimously agrees is best in its class? I've met many new artisanal food entrepreneurs who promote their brand in this way. Your close friends and relatives may think that your gooey dark chocolate brownies are simply the "best," no qualification needed. But what about the millions of people who prefer milk chocolate brownies with a cakey texture? They may interpret your confidence as false advertising...

Technologists are also (in)famous for falling in love with their own creation. "Why bother explaining how this new software is different from the old one, or finding out whether real humans actually care about this new feature? Once people get a sneak peek, they'll be falling over themselves to get it!" It's safe to say that billions of dollars and countless hours have been wasted in the creation of digital products that no one wants. The same is true of physical products, of course, but higher overhead forces non-tech entrepreneurs to be a little more mindful of their market.

Business is inherently risky; you can never guarantee that a certain product or service will excel in the complicated, ever-changing marketplace. But a little humility will go a long way in crafting a What that resonates with real customers in the real world. Remember that business is a relationship, not a transaction: communication and empathy are just as important as your offerings.

If you believe that differentiation is irrelevant to you because your product or service is the first of its kind, remember that your target customers were making do before your product or service existed. How? Unless you're in the business of life-saving medications, they managed to survive.

It's important to have respect for the resourcefulness of your target customers. Are you sure your budgeting software would make their lives easier than the customized Excel spreadsheet they've been using for years? Does your mac-and-cheese really taste better than their grandmother's simple recipe? Is your consulting service really providing insights they couldn't arrive at on their own?

Of course, the answer to how your target customers managed before you came along usually includes the products or services of other brands. This brings us to the second case: not taking competitors seriously. However different these other brands are from yours, these are your competitors, and they deserve respect. It's a big mistake to dismiss other businesses because they don't offer exactly what you offer. No matter what problem you're trying to solve or value you're trying to create, you're probably not the first. When you don't seek out competitors, you're missing out on an opportunity to learn from both the successes and failures of those who have gone before you.

Sometimes you can also be missing out on an opportunity to strategically pivot your business. I'll never forget what one entrepreneur, three years into building an organic skincare brand, said during a consultation: "I would never have gotten into this had I realized how competitive the industry is." It's daunting to find out that your business is not as special as you thought it was. It's even more daunting to feel that your success relies on being a confident salesperson in spite of your uncertainty. It's much more satisfying in the long run to face the competition head-on and figure out how to make something that's truly unique and valuable to your target customers.

Thoroughly and accurately understanding the strengths and weaknesses of your competitors (which you can only do if you acknowledge that you have them) also puts you in a much better place to compete with them. Over time, this kind of respectful competition will help you own your niche and let go of people who are not your target customers. Instead of dogmatically stating that "no one makes brownies like mine," the baker from our previous example would be able to say, "I make the gooiest brownies for dark chocolate lovers, but the bakery across town has cakey desserts if that's more your thing." That's the voice of confidence, and it sounds good. Your customers will trust you more when you're comfortable and specific about what you do and don't provide.

You don't need to have the only or best offering in your category to build a strong brand or sustainable business. Small businesses in particular don't thrive by thinking about competition in this way. Small businesses tend to thrive by being nimble, resourceful, and attuned to their target customers. They excel at doing a lot with a little. They are the Davids of the David and Goliath business world—winning battles with a slingshot and no armor. You don't have to outweigh, outmuscle or outyell other businesses. Just find your slingshot and practice your aim.

That being said, if you do happen to have an offering that's particularly unique, Godspeed! You may have more challenges than the entrepreneur who just has to explain why their brand is different from familiar alternatives. You, Dear Reader, have to educate your target customers from scratch. If anything, how you communicate about your differentiators will be more—not less—of a challenge to your brand than it is to others.

When it comes to identifying your key differentiators, start out by considering everything that makes your brand even the slightest bit different from others. You can draw from your product/service features, story, mission, brand persona, even target customers (some brands stand out just by targeting an underserved niche). From this massive list, pick a few things that a) really matter to your target customers, and b) you want to make a core part of your brand and are able to sustain in the long-term. What do you want to be known for?

Example Differentiators

- We demystify branding
- Our step-by-step process takes days, not months
- We "get" small business
- We're equally strong in strategy, copy, and design
- We cut across industry and cultural lines

Exercises

1. Where are your target customers going for help?
2. What frustrations or limitations do your target customers have with those solutions?
3. What similar brands or solutions has your target customer tried before?
4. What did your target customer like about those other brands?
5. What did your target customer not like about those other brands?

6. What do you find cool, interesting, or special about your business?

7. Is there anything unique about your top product or service?

8. Is there anything unique about your business model?

9. Is there anything unique about your operations or customer service?

10. Do a compliment audit. List everything good anyone has ever said about your brand, product/service, or business. Remember comments and read reviews. Do you see any patterns?

Core Competency

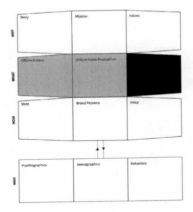

Your core competency is simply the activity your business does best.

It can be scary to name what you're best at, because it implies that you're not great at everything. And doesn't that mean you'll lose respect (and potential customers)?

When I started out as a freelance writer, I was interested in everything and didn't have a specialty. As a service provider, my overhead was low, so I was able to indulge my desire to try my hand at a plethora of projects. I wrote for many different industries—finance, nutrition, insurance, gaming, fitness, software. I wrote for different formats—blogs, websites, essays, reviews, emails, proposals, fiction, ebooks. And in fact, I often did more than just writing—some projects involved research, editing, and/or proofreading.

I don't regret my years of experimentation. They taught me what I enjoyed, what I was good at, and what the marketplace looked like for a freelance writer. But the hustle was exhausting. Because I didn't have a specialty, I had to compete with thousands of other freelancers without specialties. Because my clients weren't looking for a specialist, they weren't willing to pay the prices that a specialist could easily charge. My experimentation time was fun, and it was necessary, but it wasn't sustainable. I needed to identify my core competency.

Many small business journeys start out in a similar way as my freelance career. Whether you thought you knew exactly what you wanted to offer or knew you wanted to try out a range of offerings, a period of experimentation is healthy and good. Being open to receiving feedback and pivoting accordingly means you're not locked into a poor product-market fit. It's much better to find out what doesn't work in a matter of days or weeks than stick with something that doesn't work for years.

The problem during this phase of business is that it can stop being an experiment and start being an identity. One of the participants in a Branding 101 workshop I conducted was a hardworking baker. She pulled me aside after class to ask, "Do you think that closing my retail booth would affect my brand?" She rented a stall in a sweet but unpopular local marketplace—and was paying exponentially more in rent and payroll than she was receiving back in sales.

As a branding rather than financial expert, I'm always hesitant to give this kind of business advice (even when the answer seems obvious). So I asked how she thought the retail booth benefited her brand. "I want to be known in the community," she answered, "but honestly I hate baking pastries every morning just to stock the booth. What I really love to do is custom cakes." Her business was getting some exposure through the booth—but exposure as a bakery with cheap pastries and coffee, not a bakery with high-end custom cakes. She was spending resources she could have used to market her specialty on creating generic products she didn't even enjoy producing. Needless to say, I wholeheartedly supported her decision to shut down the unprofitable retail space.

How do you name a core competency when you have a wide variety of offerings?

First of all, consider narrowing your offerings. If the thought of only limiting yourself to what you do well and enjoy providing fills you with premonitions of bankruptcy, you're not alone. I meet many entrepreneurs who think that having a small business means they have to take whatever they can get to survive.

This simply isn't true. As a small business, it's true that you have limited resources. But limitations are funny. We often ignore them because we don't like them—I've made that mistake too many times to count. But they're only a problem when they're ignored. When we're realistic about our limits, they're a blessing. They force us to be better at what we can actually control and let go of the rest. In branding, they force us to focus on what the business can actually do and be.

Whether or not you've committed to only providing what you truly are great at providing, your business will still probably offer at least two products or services. So how do you name a core competency? The key is to let go of being literal and, instead, play around with different ideas.

If you have a restaurant, your core competency might have to do with providing a certain kind of food. Or it might have to do with providing a certain kind of experience. If you have a fashion consultancy, your core competency might have to do with choosing outfits. Or it might be about how you make clients feel. It all depends on what your particular business is particularly great at.

As a freelance writer, it took some creativity and patience to land on my core competency. The easiest route to specialization would have been to hone in on an industry and format—to become an expert in writing case studies for finance companies, for example. But defining my niche in this traditional way felt stifling to me. It would be much more profitable but much less sustainable psychologically. One thing I learned about myself during the experimentation phase was that I loved helping clients from different industries create different types of content. I enjoyed the challenge of understanding both the client's and their target customer's perspective. I loved translating the client's message into something that made sense to the reader—and I was good at it.

After analyzing the experiences I'd had during my experimentation phase, I realized that my value as a freelancer did not need to come from my superior technical skills or industry knowledge. In fact, my superpowers lay in my soft skills (like problem-solving and empathy) and what I did not know. Instead of writing dense technical material for a specific audience, I made a niche out of writing engaging, jargon-free content for readers who, like me, knew little about the client's brand or industry at first. This expertise is a lot more valuable to small business owners (my target customers) than expertise in writing finance case studies. And I enjoyed doing it a lot more too!

There are many ways to frame your core competency. While it may seem scary or limiting at first, keep an open mind. Owning a niche is essential to standing out and being profitable in a crowded marketplace over time, but it doesn't have to be rushed or forced. Consider it a chance to celebrate what your business is good at, and a chance to reduce the time you spend on things you don't enjoy. It's liberating to know that you're great at something you both enjoy and that really helps the humans you love to serve.

Example Core Competency

Strengthening small business brands using a streamlined, emotionally intelligent process

Exercises

1. What do you currently offer customers?
2. How would you describe what connects all your offerings?
3. What problems do you solve for your target customer?

4. What emotional benefits are you giving your target customer?
5. What do you most enjoy selling?
6. What is your business consistently great at?
7. What makes you and/or your team great at what you do?
8. What product or service would you most want the world to know about?

Unique Value Proposition

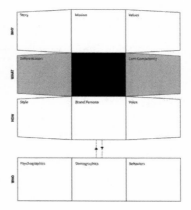

Your unique value proposition is what makes your brand better than any other—in the eyes of your target customer.

Value propositions are a big deal in business and marketing. Like marriage propositions, they are offerings meant to attract the attention and commitment of a mate: your target customer. A value proposition is a pitch, the reason a product or service is right for a certain buyer.

Without a value proposition, your product or service is just that: a thing or an action without context or meaning. What need or desire does that thing or action fulfill? Couples don't get married to exchange rings, but rings are exchanged when couples get married. Your product or service is the ring. What matters more than the size of the stone is the long-term relationship it represents.

Value propositions are at the heart of marketing because value creation is the core of business. It's only natural that a unique value proposition is at the center of your brand. It's what enables your business to stand out among all the other suitors and win the heart of your target customer.

A quick side note on value propositions for your products and services. Every one of your offerings should have its own value proposition. You might even have different value propositions for different customers. Like an elevator pitch, a value proposition should be flexible enough to adjust to the context. What we're doing by naming your brand's unique value proposition is identifying the cornerstone of all those other value propositions. The challenge is to think beyond your products and services to what value your entire business offers.

So how do you define what makes your brand uniquely valuable to your target customer? You've already done half the work. To craft your UVP, start with your core competency, mix in your key differentiators, then strain it through the lens of what matters to your target customer.

Your brand's unique value proposition is a deceptively simple answer to a very complex question. Your brand probably includes multiple products and/or services, each with their own set of features and benefits. It also includes all the elements of your Why (Story, Mission, Values) and How (Style, Brand Personality, Voice). How do you know which of these features, benefits, or brand elements to emphasize?

Many entrepreneurs, especially those who have created their key product or technology themselves, bristle at the idea of naming THE unique value proposition of their brand. "My brand is unique in every way," they might say. "And it offers multiple value propositions for dozens of target customers!"

If that's you, consider this: The human brain is incredibly efficient. It's processing tons of data every second and 'prunes' away everything that doesn't seem extremely relevant to its current goals. In other words, it's obsessed with simplification. That's true of your brain, and it's true of your customers' brains, and there's nothing you can do about it. So why swim against the tide?

Naming a single unique value proposition doesn't mean your brand offers only that value. It means that you're so committed to providing that value that no matter what, come hell or high water, your customer will receive that value, gosh darn it.

This is the reason others have described a unique value proposition as a "brand promise." Some have even gone so far as to say that a brand is that promise. A promise is not whatever feature, benefit, value, or personality trait a business happens to emphasize this year, or that happens to appeal to customers on a given day. A promise is a vow, a solemn contract. It's not something you forget or experiment with. It's the foundation of trust between you and your customer.

Some small businesses don't have a unique value proposition, and they still survive. Unfortunately, they might not last long. Having a value proposition that isn't unique is a dangerous thing. At any time, another brand can come along with something just slightly better and win over the same customers. There's no incentive to be loyal, nothing that makes that brand feel perfect for me.

But that won't be the story of your business, because you're going to name and own that value proposition that's unique to your business and resonates with your target customer. It won't be as hard as it seems, because you've already done much of the work! The reason we're only talking about the unique value proposition at the end of the What section is that your differentiators and core competency directly feed into your UVP.

Your job will be to pinpoint what makes your core competency especially valuable to your target market. Then you'll figure out which of your differentiators are especially interesting or important to your target market. Finally, you'll piece together those two elements into a coherent, compelling statement that captures the very heart of your business and brand.

Example Unique Value Proposition

Sunbird Creative is a boutique agency that builds brands real humans love—within days, not months.

Exercises

1. What's the best feedback you've gotten on your products/services in the past?
2. How does your business make life better for your target customers?
3. What feature of your product or service immediately attract your target customer?
4. Which one or two of your differentiators do your target customers care most about?
5. If your brand were only ever known for one thing, what would you want that one thing to be?
6. Try formulating your UVP using each of the following value proposition templates:
   - Geoff Moore's Value Positioning Statement (edited): For [target customer] who [statement of the need or opportunity], our brand is [category] that [statement of benefit].
   - Steve Blank's XYZ: We help X do Y by doing Z.
   - Dave McClure's Elevator Ride: Simple phrases describing what + how + why.
   - Eric Sink's Value Positioning (edited): The most [superlative] [brand type] for [target customer].

Key Takeaways

- The What of your Brand Canvas answers the question, "What are your superpowers?"
- Your unique value proposition (UVP) is what makes your brand perfect for your target customer.
- Your core competency is the thing your brand is best at.
- Your differentiators are the ways your brand stands out from the crowd.
- To define your UVP, blend your core competency and your differentiators, then strain it through the lens of what matters to your target customer.
- Your unique value proposition is at the center of your small business brand. A clear understanding of your UVP will turbocharge your marketing efforts.
- Trying to be everything to everybody is tiring and ineffective. However, those who go through the painful process of embracing their limitations come out the other side with the most joy and strongest brands.
- Defining your What comes with great power and great responsibility. The process requires you to admit what you're not great at and where your brand doesn't stand out, so that you can embrace the special powers only your brand has.

HOW

WHY	Story	Mission	Values
WHAT	Differentiators	Unique Value Proposition	Core Competency
HOW	Style	Brand Persona	Voice
WHO	Psychographics	Demographics	Behaviors

91

How does your brand look and sound?

Your "How" is the unique way your business communicates with target customers, the way it presents itself to the world. Your How is comprised of three elements:

- Style
- Brand Persona
- Voice

If your brand were a person, these would be the equivalent of their role and personality type (persona), their unique look and manner (style), and the way they speak (voice). In other words, it's the fun stuff.

Why Your "How" Matters

It may seem strange that we've taken so long, in a book about branding, to get to the topics of persona and style. But if you were just interested in slapping a cool look on top of your business, you would probably be reading another book or (let's be real) a how-to blog post. There's tons of content out there all about design, voice, and brand persona. You chose this book because you wanted to understand how it all fits together.

Here's what you need to know: How you look and sound is the first thing customers notice, but it's the last step of a good branding process. That's because developing a brand persona before understanding your Who, Why, and What is like shopping for an outfit for a complete stranger. If you don't know anything about their lifestyle, preferences, budget, or culture, where do you even start? You'll probably default to getting them something trendy, or something you happen to like. Which is exactly how many people approach branding.

Developing a brand persona, expressed in language and design, is not more important than your mission or unique value proposition. But it does have a more immediate impact. Just as we notice the way a stranger looks or sounds long before getting to know who they are, your target customers notice how you communicate your message before understanding the content of your message. In a fraction of a second, they'll draw conclusions about your brand. They might even decide, right there and then, whether your brand is right for them—based on nothing but an instinctive reaction to a first impression. And they won't even know they're doing it.

While we like to think of ourselves as rational creatures, it's well-established in cognitive science that over 90% of our thought processes take place beneath the level of our self-awareness and self-control. Our conscious selves are like "riders" on what psychologist Jonathan Haidt calls the "elephants" of our unconscious mind. No matter how articulately we explain our decisions after we've made them, we are almost always pulled by forces deep within us that we barely understand.

Studies have shown that getting educated—even in statistics, logic, or psychology—has no effect on this tendency. We can get better at rationalizing our decisions and even at seeing flaws in others' decision-making, but we haven't discovered a way to become fundamentally more rational in our own decision-making. Our brains are simply more elephant than rider.

This fact about human brains—that our thoughts and decisions are almost totally unconscious and intuitive—is the reason branding is so powerful.

On the Brand Canvas, you'll notice that your How (persona, style, and voice) are closer to the target customer than your What and Why. That's because it's both the first thing they'll notice and the filter through which they will interact with the other elements. Brand persona colors how you tell your story, what you're communicating about your differentiators (intentionally and unintentionally), whether your mission seems authentic, and so on.

When you're clear about your Who, Why, and What, decisions

about your brand persona, style, and voice tend to flow naturally. In our work with small business owners, Mara and I have never come across a business whose main challenge was their How. Many entrepreneurs seek branding help because they (very naturally) want a more memorable logo or punchier web copy. But there is always something deeper going on. While we spend a lot of time designing and writing for our clients, the bulk of our problem solving happens before we touch voice or style.

First we had to figure out who our own agency's target customer really was. We realized that the location and gender of our best clients mattered less than their habits and personality. Then we could adjust our services (to reach customers beyond New York), our language (to speak directly to mission-oriented entrepreneurs), and our style (to emphasize our intelligence and tech-savviness more than our down-to-earth approachability).

First we had to discover that BBT's ambitious mission and deep commitment to diversity, equity, and inclusion differentiated the collective from other firms doing organizational development. From there we could craft the brand's persona as bold but grounded, empathetic but goal-oriented. And then we could translate that personality into a warm and lively visual identity full of geometric forms, as well as a confident, positive voice.

First we had to position Massawa as NYC's oldest African eatery, inviting patrons to enjoy Eritrean-Ethiopian food in a relaxed, contemporary setting. Then we could craft an approachable, quirky, and culturally sensitive brand persona that would capture Massawa's unique flavor. And then we could create a color scheme for both their marketing materials and restaurant, minimalist illustrations based on Eritrean art, and simple language that warmly welcomed strangers and friends to make themselves at home at the restaurant.

There's not one right way to translate brand persona into style and voice. An imaginative brand could have a minimalist style and bold voice—or it could have a whimsical style and gentle voice. But agreeing on the traits you want the style and voice to communicate does limit your options, making it easier to be consistent and strategic. A brand that wants to be known as imaginative should probably avoid a traditional style and serious voice.

Your brand's How is as fun to flesh out as it is important to think about. When you know who your humans are, why your business exists, and what your superpowers are, you can enjoy the process of creating a persona, style, and voice even more—because you know at each step whether you're heading in the right direction or not. You're able to communicate more easily with designers and writers. And you'll now find new ways to enhance every part of your customer's experience, from finding out about your product or service to making their 10th purchase.

Brand Persona

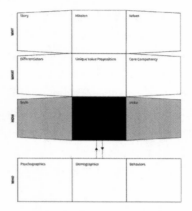

Brand Persona is what makes your brand feel human. It's a description of the distinctive identity of your business as if it were a person in relationship with your customer—rather than a 'business entity' in relationship with a 'market.' Your persona is made up of three elements:

1. Your brand's role (in relationship to your target customer)
2. Your brand's personality traits
3. The way your brand wants to make your target customer feel

Articulating your brand persona helps you flesh out your brand in a way that enables people to experience something tangible and familiar when they interact with it. Persona is a big part of what makes your brand feel real and alive. Being consistent with your persona helps your brand feel trustworthy.

The key to creating a brand persona is to see your brand as a human being, someone who plays a certain role, with distinct personality traits and clear desires. Specificity is key! When you're done, you should be able to easily imagine a real person from the description in the Brand Persona box.

The implications of your persona become clear once you compare alternatives. Consider an athletic shoe brand introducing a new product. The brand's persona will affect nearly everything about the way the product is presented. Consider the way these three personas might advertise differently:

- An intense coach who wants to make you feel motivated
- A carefree friend who wants to make you feel relaxed
- An encouraging parent who wants to make you feel unique

These three people would naturally pitch the same shoe in different ways. Try to match each of the above personas with one of the descriptions of a poster ad below.

- A retro photo of a group of friends having a picnic on a soccer field with the text: "Kick (back) with these."
- A photo of three diverse teenagers wearing totally different outfits (except for the same shoes) beneath neon letters that read: "Do your thing."
- A black-and-white close-up photo of a sweaty runner about to launch off the starting blocks with the caption: "Do you have what it takes to make it to the finish line?"

It's easy to feel how different these three ads are—and much harder to explain why. Persona helps you quickly and intuitively make decisions about design and language that communicate your message like a real human. Identifying a persona is a way to make brand Style and Voice concrete. With a persona in mind, you can tap into vivid language and imagery, and avoid the trap of seeming cold and generic.

1. Role

Humans exist in relationship with other humans. Your brand's role describes the kind of person your brand would be in society. Is your brand more of a friend or a teacher? A white-collar professional or a stay-at-home parent? A tour guide or an explorer?

Naming your role is an imaginative exercise that will help you think creatively as you craft a brand that feels human. The way your brand looks and speaks will remind your customers of something. The goal of naming your brand's role is to remind them on an unconscious, visceral level of a specific kind of person—ideally someone they know and like. Unlike your Mission and Unique Value Proposition, your role is not literal and does not need to be expressed to your customers.

2. Personality

The magical thing about brand personality is that it can infuse, humanize, and elevate every customer-touching aspect of your business. Apple's cool, innovative brand personality certainly affects their product design. Zappos's ultra-friendly personality comes through in downright enjoyable phone calls with well-trained customer service reps. And, on the other side, Volkswagon's supposedly reliable brand took a major hit when the world found out that they were fudging their emissions tests.

There are several different theories of what traits make up a personality that we won't get into in this book. If you're interested in psychology or particularly dedicated to making your brand personality more human, I highly recommend researching the following theories. Becoming familiar with different models of human personality will give you the lenses to start seeing new patterns in yourself, friends, and others. As you practice identifying traits in people according to these models, you'll break out of old ways of thinking about personality and be much better prepared to extend that new awareness to brands.

The MBTI: My personal favorite, the Myers-Briggs (or MBTI) identifies sixteen personality types based on combinations of eight traits (or "functions"). What I find incredible about the Myers-Briggs model is how well it predicts the strengths and challenges of not only each type, but of the relationships between types. Its ability to improve relationships may be why it's been the most popular personality tool within business for decades.

Sally Hogshead's Advantages: Created by a veteran brand strategist, this model identifies seven strengths that both people and brands can tap into to captivate their audience. In her book Fascinate: How to Make Your Brand Impossible to Resist, Hogshead identifies these seven "Advantages" as Innovation, Passion, Power, Prestige, Mystique, Alert, and Trust. If describing your brand personality feels overwhelming to you, this is a fantastic place to start.

Traditional models: One of the most well-established models within psychology is the Big Five, which describes personalities as unique combinations of five distinct traits (extraversion, agreeableness, neuroticism, openness, and conscientiousness). One of the most ancient models is the Enneagram, a model of nine interrelated types. The spiritually-based Enneagram is popular in self-help and personal growth literature.

You can find plenty more about each of these personality models online, as well as free self-assessments.

Speaking of self-assessments... how much should your brand's personality match your own? This question comes up a lot for personal brands and microbusinesses, but it applies to every type of brand. Behind every brand there is, after all, at least one human.

Solopreneurs have one of two tendencies: a) to try to fit all of their personality into the brand (as if it were an extension of themselves), or b) to try to remove their personality from the brand completely (as if their business were totally separate from themselves). While the appropriate amount of transparency is different for everyone, a good rule of thumb is to selectively include elements of your actual personality into your brand.

When Mara and I started Sunbird Creative, we had to figure out which of our personality traits to bring to the brand. We learned a lot about ourselves and each other in the process. As long-time friends who often felt deeply connected and uncommonly similar, it was fascinating to realize how many differences there were between us. While we're both creative, I gravitate toward anything unique and original, while Mara embraces tradition and prioritizes excellence. While we're both thoughtful and reflective, I am future-oriented and Mara is focused on the present. While we're both compassionate, I like to serve people through teaching and Mara prefers listening.

It took over a year of working together for us to understand our similarities, differences, and what traits our target customers responded well to. Because it's such a personal process, especially for a service business, it was frustrating and disorienting at times. But it was also deeply satisfying and clarifying. When we hear clients describe us using some of the exact words in our Brand Canvas, we know that the process was worth it.

Not sure which traits to choose? Imagine yourself hiring a team. What characteristics would you look for in a candidate (beyond the integrity to show up on time, work hard, and avoid stealing food from the fridge)? How would you teach them how to interact with customers in a way that represents your brand well? How would you explain the 'vibe' you're going for in new marketing materials?

If you do in fact have a team, you've already dealt with these questions to some degree. They're not easy to answer, and you might find yourself leaving brand personality to chance or defaulting to generic terms like "helpful" and "professional." If that's you, there's an opportunity waiting for you to make your business even more meaningful by consciously transferring some of your own quirks and passions into the brand. Good business, branding, and customer service doesn't have to be about checking all the right boxes and doing things perfectly. There's room to be human. Your customers want to be served—but they also want to connect with you on a personal level.

Two quick notes on terminology. First, you'll sometimes see brand personality referred to as "brand identity." This is a bit misleading. Personality is so much a part of who we are that it's hard to think about our identities as separate from our personalities. But just like you are more than just a collection of human personality traits, brands are more than a collection of brand personality traits. And just like everything you do—from the way you cook an egg to the way you walk across a room—is affected by your personality, human brands let personality affect everything.

Second, it can be difficult to distinguish between personality and Values in your Brand Canvas. Just like a human's personality can be difficult to distinguish from their character. We know the difference intuitively, but they tend to blend together in our minds. One helpful way to separate brand personality from brand values is to ask the questions: "What is my brand like?" and "What does my brand care about?" A person who cares about the environment might be quiet and reserved, or they may be loud and energetic. But you wouldn't describe their personality as "environmentalistic."

3. Emotional effect

The final piece of your Brand Persona is the main emotion you want your brand to inspire in your target customers. Naturally, any relationship will draw out different emotions at different times— often multiple emotions at once. Your customers will have complex associations with your brand. But when you name the emotion you most want them to feel, as much of the time as possible, you'll be able to be even more strategic and creative with your design and language. And you might find it easier, with a goal in mind, to continue to think of both your brand and your target customer as humans.

Example Brand Persona

We are a passionate young professor who wants to make you feel refreshed.

Exercises

1. What other brands are most like yours (or would you want yours to be like)? If they were a person, how would you describe them?
2. What other brands are least like yours (or would you hate yours to be like)? If they were a person, how would you describe them?
3. If your brand were a famous person, who would it be and why?
4. If your brand were a fictional character, who would it be and why?
5. If your brand were a person, who would it be in relationship with your target customer? Choose from among the following or create your own:
   - Friend
   - Teacher
   - Lover
   - Parent
   - Mentor
   - Acquaintance
6. To start zooming in on your brand's traits, pick one of the following words from each of the pairs below:
   - Adventurous or safe
   - Easygoing or intense
   - Calm or enthusiastic
   - Charismatic or reserved
   - Cheerful or serious
   - Competitive or cooperative
   - Creative or meticulous
   - Curious or focused

- o Diligent or imaginative
- o Empathetic or opinionated
- o Efficient or patient
- o Insightful or procedural
- o Persuasive or open-minded
- o Organized or intuitive
- o Perceptive or resourceful
- o Stable or dynamic
- o Youthful or wise
- o Dramatic or reliable
- o Fierce or warm
- o Flirty or straightforward
- o Eccentric or traditional
- o Delicate or powerful
- o Hip or old-school
- o Active or reflective
- o Resourceful or prepared
- o Sensitive or confident
- o Scholarly or athletic
- o Idealistic or no-nonsense

7. How do you want to make target customers feel? Pick one each of the two-word pairs below.
    - o Secure or inspired
    - o Energetic or relaxed
    - o Light-hearted or competent
    - o Intrigued or connected
    - o Powerful or tender
    - o Content or motivated
    - o Optimistic or realistic

8. Try describing your Brand Persona using the following template:
    - o We are a [personality trait] [role] who wants to make you feel [emotion].

Style

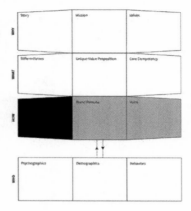

Style describes how your Brand Persona presents itself to the world. It's your persona translated into a visual language, the look and feel of your brand.

Because human brains process images many times faster than words, your brand's Style is often the part of your brand that a target customer first comes into contact with. It's often the part that makes a first impression and leads them to draw conclusions about your brand persona.

The speed at which we process visual information makes style even more difficult to talk about than personality traits. In addition to being unaware of 90% of our thought processes, most of us are not trained to talk about what we see. Unless you've attended art classes or work in a creative field, you probably haven't had many opportunities to identify how the specific use of elements like light, color, and negative space in an image communicates certain meanings and evokes certain feelings. When talking about visual design, it's much easier to talk about whether we like it or not than it is to explain why.

Unless you have a background in design, describing your brand's style may be the most confusing part of the Brand Canvas process. Don't expect to nail it perfectly. In fact, I encourage you to see it as an exercise in appreciating the difficulty of a professional designer's day-to-day challenges. Even as someone who has worked closely with a graphic designer for years, I still struggle to put words to my thoughts about design.

Thankfully, experienced designers can help people like us translate jumbled thoughts into meaningful style language. They can also help you see the different ways your brand persona could be translated into a brand style—and what styles don't match the personality you want to convey. They do this by asking questions that spark your imagination and get you to describe your brand from different angles. They're able to reverse-engineer a style from the emotions you want to evoke and the impression you want to leave.

The words you use in the Style box of your Brand Canvas will become the basis for your brand's style guidelines. Your brand's style will be most evident in your marketing materials and other customer touchpoints, such as your:

- Website
- Physical location
- Print materials
- Ads
- Promotional emails
- Product packaging
- Product design
- Social media profiles

When you think about all these different ways your target customers interact with your business, you can see how difficult it is to create a consistent impression throughout their interactions with you. While creating your Brand Canvas will guarantee that your brand's style flows naturally from the rest of your brand, you'll need style guidelines to translate that style into the real world.

Creating style guidelines will ensure your brand is presented in a coherent way in all different formats. Consistency is absolutely essential to appearing trustworthy and being remembered. A unique style that communicates the brand persona and appeals deeply to your target customer will not do much for your brand if you only sometimes or usually use it. At best, inconsistency in your brand style is a missed opportunity to make a strong impression. At worst, it can make your whole brand seem unprofessional and untrustworthy.

If you're operating with no guidelines at all right now, start out by keeping it really simple. We have a resource in our online store (look for The Style Guide Toolkit at sunbirdcreative.com/toolkits) to help you use your description to create a one-page sheet that captures the essentials of your brand's Style:

- Your logo
- 1-2 brand colors (with Hex codes)
- 2 fonts (one for headers and one for regular font)

Many small businesses underestimate the importance of style consistency. Just by using the same logo, colors, and fonts in all of your touchpoints, you will stand out from the countless businesses that aren't thoughtful about their brand.

Example Style:

- Minimalism with soul
- Clean look with warm details
- Modern with a feminine touch

Exercises

1. If your brand were a place, what place would it be?
2. If your brand were a person, what kind of clothes would it wear? Why?
3. Imagine you could afford any office/retail/restaurant space you could dream of. Where is it? What does it look like, smell like,

feel like?

4. Choose up to 10 words that best describe your brand's look and feel:

Adorable	Efficient	Industrial
Adventurous	Elegant	Informal
Artistic	Endearing	Innovative
Athletic	Energetic	Inspiring
Bold	Ethereal	Intense
Bright	Exciting	Inviting
Busy	Familiar	Low-Maintenance
Calm	Efficient	Lively
Caring	Elegant	Lush
Casual	Endearing	Majestic
Charming	Energetic	Modern
Cheerful	Ethereal	Natural
Chic	Exciting	No-nonsense
Classic	Familiar	Nostalgic
Colorful	Fashionable	Old
Comfortable	Festive	Organic
Conservative	Fierce	Playful
Cool	Flirty	Professional
Creative	Formal	Quaint
Cutting-Edge	Fresh	Quirky
Daring	Friendly	Radiant
Dazzling	Fun	Rebellious
Delicate	Functional	Relaxing
Delightful	Futuristic	Reliable
Detailed	Glamorous	Retro
Dramatic	Graceful	Revolutionary
Earthy	Hip	Romantic
Eccentric	Historic	Royal
Rustic	Stimulating	Trustworthy

Scholarly	Straightforward	Unconventional
Serious	Striking	Upbeat
Silly	Strong	Urban
Sleek	Stylish	Vintage
Smart	Swanky	Whimsical
Soothing	Tasteful	Wild
Sophisticated	Tranquil	Youthful
Stable		

Voice

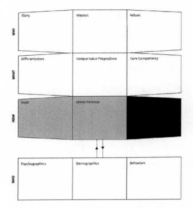

Voice is the translation of your Brand Persona into the way your brand sounds.

I have yet to meet a small business owner who already has written voice guidelines (often called editorial or content style guidelines). While most entrepreneurs believe in the visceral power of design and the persuasive power of words, few realize how much impact how a brand says things can have. I don't blame them. In some ways it's easier to talk about something as concrete as a logo or an elevator pitch than something as vague as voice.

The goal of the Voice section of your Brand Canvas is to create guidelines for the specific words and tone your brand uses. These should match and express your Brand Persona. Voice affects every piece of your marketing that contains words—that is to say, almost everything, including:

- Websites
- Print materials
- Ads
- Packaging
- Emails (all types)

- Social media posts
- Sales pitches
- In-person presentations
- Blog posts

Consciously or unconsciously, people will hear a speaker with a specific tone behind all the language your brand uses. A brand with a strong voice sounds like a real person because it uses specific words and appropriate tones based on a clear persona.

Most small business owners tend to err on the side of sounding generic. It can seem safer to use vague or "professional" language than say something very specific in a very specific way. No one wants to turn potential customers off! But of course, now that you know who your target customers are, you don't need to worry about everyone else. You're ready to speak like a human to humans.

Developing a clear Voice gives you the power to use words even more persuasively and effectively. As with Brand Persona and Style, simply thinking about Voice puts you ahead of your competitors and enables you to see other brands with sharper lenses.

In a genius piece of stand-up, comedian Trevor Noah imagines a meeting between a young Barack Obama and a seasoned Nelson Mandela. Obama, who has not yet achieved political success, is thrilled to meet his hero. He expresses his adoration in a gush of high-pitched words: "I want to be just like you, man, I read all your books and I saw what you were doing in prison and I was like, I want to be the first black president of America and do the same thing you did…"

Mandela interrupts to answer, "Not with that voice!"

For the next four minutes, Trevor Noah enacts a hilarious scene in which Mandela becomes Obama's voice coach. Finally the young Barack transforms himself from an idealistic kid into an icon of stability and gravitas—through just his voice. It's amazing how powerful the effect of this change is. Deep, slow voices simply feel presidential in a way that a squeaky, high-pitched voice never could!

How we say words is often as important as the actual words we use. While few people think much about tone on a daily basis, we are constantly using it to interpret other people's motives, thoughts, and feelings. Certain tones appeal to us and others turn us off.

Imagine you've just ordered an expensive drink at a café. Just before turning away, you notice a tip jar and decide to drop in your change—all ten cents. The cashier says, "Thanks." How would you interpret that interaction? It depends on their tone. Maybe it was a mechanical response, without much feeling (as in, "Thanks. Next customer!"). Maybe it was sarcastic (as in, "Thanks for your huge tip…"). Or maybe it was a heartfelt appreciation for your thoughtfulness (as in, "Thanks so much for being generous and considerate!")

The Voice box of your Brand Canvas will include adjectives that are the foundation of your brand's language. More detailed guidelines may be useful, especially if you rely heavily on written content or thought leadership for marketing. While there are no universally used language guidelines (also known as editorial, content, or writing style guidelines), we use a simple template at Sunbird Creative you can find as part of the Brand Identity Toolkit at sunbirdcreative.com/toolkits. Our Language Guide includes:

- Slogan/tagline
- Persona
- Tone words, with do's and don'ts for each
- Boilerplate company description
- Important terminology
- Grammar and mechanics

The key to a strong brand voice is making it concrete, consistent, and specific. Keep playing with different ways to describe tone until you can practically hear your brand's voice in your ear. The purpose of the How section of your Brand Canvas is to make your brand more trustworthy and relatable. Generic voices are for faceless corporations, not powerful small businesses with authentic brands.

Example Voice

- Smart but approachable
- Confident but not pushy
- Gentle but direct

Exercises

1. If your brand were a person, how would you describe its physical voice? Choose one from each of the following pairs.
   o Male or female
   o High or low
   o Gravelly or smooth
   o Accented or unaccented
   o Monotone or expressive

2. Look back at your Brand Persona. What tone would that person tend to use? Choose one from each of the following word pairs to help home in on a few words.
   o Amused or sympathetic
   o Formal or informal
   o Self-assured or modest
   o Lively or restrained
   o Witty or straightforward
   o Clinical or fanciful
   o Blunt or diplomatic
   o Reverent or irreverent
   o Urgent or easygoing
   o Emotional or matter-of-fact
   o Silly or serious
   o Didactic or reflective
   o Candid or complimentary

3. Which of the previous tones would your brand never use? Why?

Key Takeaways

- The How section of your Brand Canvas answers the question, "How does your brand look and sound?"
- More than any other step in the branding process, it's vital to think about your brand as a human when fleshing out your Brand Persona.
- Embrace the unique aspects of your brand's personality, but don't be different just for the sake of being different. Your Brand Persona does not have to be a major differentiator of your brand. Defining a persona is about being strategic, not "cool."
- To be authentic and easy to maintain, your brand personality should reflect some part of your human personality. At the same time, your small business brand (even if it's ultimately a personal brand) is not you. Choose a handful of your actual traits that appeal to your target customers, and make sure those traits come through in all of your communications.
- Style describes how your brand looks and feels. Your style words form the basis of your brand's Style Guide.
- Voice describes how your brand sounds, including your persona and tone. Your voice is the foundation of your brand's Language Guide.
- Your brand's style and voice should flow naturally from its personality.
- When it comes to Brand Persona, Style, and Voice, being consistent can be harder to achieve than being unique. But consistency is more important than uniqueness when it comes to earning trust and credibility. If you're new to branding, keep your personality traits and guidelines simple at first so you're able to implement them effectively.

PUTTING IT ALL TOGETHER

You've learned the theory behind effective human branding. You've delved into every aspect of your own brand. You've answered difficult questions about yourself and your business.

You have all the raw material to put together your own Brand Canvas. Up to this point, you've thought about each aspect of your brand separately. It's time to bring it all together and create a streamlined brand identity in which each piece fits seamlessly.

The Brand Canvas Layout

Pull out a blank Brand Canvas. (If you need fresh templates, head to sunbirdcreative.com/toolkits to download the Brand Canvas Toolkit.) Now that you know what each box is all about, you'll see how the layout of the Brand Canvas contains clues about how they fit together.

The three sections in the upper portion of the Brand Canvas (Why, What, and How) capture your brand; the lower section (Who) captures your target customer.

The center box of each section represents the core of that section. The soul of your brand is its Mission. The heart of your brand is its Unique Value Proposition. The face of your brand is its personality.

Why is at the top of the Brand Canvas because it's where the business started and what keeps it going—mostly behind the scenes. The Why tends to be less obvious to your target customer than your What and How. Many businesses never explicitly state their mission, story, or values to their target customer (although they're missing out on an opportunity to connect).

What is at the center of the Brand Canvas because it's where your business strategy, marketing strategy, and brand strategy overlap. Your unique value proposition is what ultimately drives your target customer to buy from you. You can have a powerful mission and ultra-engaging brand personality and still have a terrible business. A value proposition that differentiates you, and that you can really deliver, is the key to a sustainable brand with loyal customers.

How is closest to the target customer because it's usually the first thing people notice. Your Brand Persona—expressed through Style (design) and Voice (words)—is among the most powerful tools you have because it creates an immediate and largely unconscious impression. It's also located below the Why and What because it's the filter through which the other components of your brand get expressed.

A strong brand won't just have interesting ideas and compelling language in each box of its Brand Canvas. Like your body's own intricate skeletal structure, the elements of a brand should fit together in a way that really works. Each element clearly connects with every other piece—not in a static or rigid way, but in a way that makes sense and is flexible enough to allow your brand to grow and breathe.

Filling Out Your Brand Canvas

Gather together all your notes and answers to the questions in this book. Whether you wrote an essay per question or just noted a few key ideas per section, it may seem daunting to turn these raw thoughts into a polished Brand Canvas.

In our Brand Canvas Toolkit, you'll find two different templates that you can use, based on what you find most helpful:

1. Blank—for those who think best with a blank canvas.
2. Lines—for those who like a little nudge and a few visual cues.

Keep in mind that the Brand Canvas is a living document. It's a tool to help you be strategic and consistent, so you can build a brand that humans love. It's not a set of rules from on high, and it shouldn't feel like a straightjacket. Use it to organize your thoughts and capture your current brand identity to the best of your ability.

You'll update your Brand Canvas regularly as you try new things and get more feedback. Revision every six to twelve months is a good thing; it means you're paying attention to what's really going on with your brand and staying proactive. Branding is an iterative process. As long as your business is alive and growing, your brand should be developing and maturing.

Now that you understand how it's designed, you have the power to make the Brand Canvas your own. You are the expert on your business—and now you're the expert on your brand! The Brand Canvas is your tool now. How you use it is ultimately up to you.

That being said, here are some tips that may help you create the first iteration of your Brand Canvas.

Aim right. As you fill in the Brand Canvas, remember that your goal is to create a brand that your target customers love, not a brand that has no problems. Growing up, my dad often repeated a quote that's commonly attributed to Voltaire: "The perfect is the enemy of the good." Confucius said it another way: "Better a diamond with a flaw than a pebble without." Your brand already has superpowers. Your job is not to pretend it doesn't also have weaknesses but to name, clarify, and own what makes it amazing.

Prioritize the present. Whether you've just started your business or have been growing it for decades, you have hopes for what your brand could become. Vision is important, but there's a risk in making your Brand Canvas too aspirational. If the gap between what you say your brand is and what other people believe it is becomes too big, you will eventually lose the trust of your target customers. It's ok to add some aspirational elements in your Brand Canvas (such as an edgier personality) if you're ready to commit to being consistent with that element (rather than alternating between edginess and subtlety). But don't worry about the ways your brand could be better. Focus on describing why it's already great.

Play around. Each box in the Brand Canvas is small for a reason. The restricted space forces you to be clear and simple. It takes a lot of clarity to come up with a concise description of something as complex as mission statement, value proposition, or brand persona. By limiting yourself to language you can fit in these boxes, you're forcing yourself to prioritize and streamline. The way to not drive yourself crazy in the process is to stay creative and open-minded. Here are a few techniques for getting the juices flowing. Use one or all of them in your own process.

Before reviewing any of your previous answers, take out a blank paper or word document and write the first three ideas that come to mind for every section of the Brand Canvas. Letting whatever you happen to remember come to the surface in this way can give you clues about what's most important or most interesting about your brand.

Read over all your notes and exercises with a highlighter, marking every word or phrase that stands out to you. Then collect these words on a separate document. Do you see any patterns? Sometimes certain ideas come up over and over again. Make sure you include these in your final Brand Canvas.

If you've been using a computer to take notes and do the exercises, get physical. Print out the Brand Canvas and write on it. Simply moving from screen to paper can jumpstart clarity and creativity.

Create three totally different versions of your Brand Canvas and pull your favorite ideas from each. This is especially useful if you've noticed that your brand could go in a few different directions (such as significantly different target customers or unique value propositions).

Polishing Your Brand Canvas

Once you have a draft of your Canvas, how do you know if it will work in the real world? There's no other way to answer that question than by testing it. The best ideas can fall flat once they meet the inevitable chaos of reality.

Your Brand Canvas will need updating as you find out what works and what doesn't, what makes sense and what doesn't, what's easy to implement and what's not. Thankfully the goal is not perfection. The goal is to stay focused and organized as you develop a strong brand.

If you're itching to apply your new clarity to your real-world business as soon as possible, go ahead! You can fine tune your Canvas after you've tested your ideas and have gotten feedback from real humans.

If you're the kind of person who gains confidence from feeling prepared, use the following checklist to ensure your Brand Canvas is ready to go. As a bonus, get a partner or someone else who knows you and your brand well to answer the same questions. Once you've checked all the boxes, you can rest assured that you're on the right path to building a brand that humans love.

Overall

☐ Does the Brand Canvas seem true to the current brand?
☐ Do all the sections feel coherent and consistent with each other?
☐ Do you feel you understand the business just from the language used in the Brand Canvas?

Who

- ☐ Do the characteristics in the Who section describe a set of real humans?
- ☐ Are the Psychographics specific enough to affect the sales and marketing strategy?
- ☐ Are the Demographic characteristics all relevant to the business?
- ☐ Does the list of Behaviors fit the type of person described by the psychographics and demographics?

Why

- ☐ From this section, does it seem that the brand cares about more than the bottom line?
- ☐ Does the Story highlight details that the target customer would find interesting?
- ☐ Is the mission relevant to the business model and products/services?
- ☐ Do the values flow naturally from the Story and Mission?

What

- ☐ Does the What section paint a picture of a confident, unique business?
- ☐ Does each differentiator truly set the business apart from others?
- ☐ Is the unique value proposition specific and clear?
- ☐ Does the target customer care about the Unique Value Proposition?
- ☐ Is the core competency specific?

How

- ☐ Does the brand persona sound like a real human?
- ☐ Would the brand persona appeal to the target customer?
- ☐ Do both the style and voice flow intuitively out of the brand persona?

☐   Is the style section specific enough that you could tell if a certain design matches it or not?

☐   Is the voice section specific enough that you could tell if a certain blog post matches it or not?

Maintaining Your Brand Canvas

Once you have your polished Brand Canvas v1.0, make sure you honor all your hard work by actually using it! The process of creating a Brand Canvas is invaluable in itself. But the tool will be most useful if you refer to it every time you make a decision about your brand.

Launching a marketing campaign? Start with your Unique Value Proposition. Not sure which product or service to feature? Refer to your core competency. Preparing for a networking event? Brush up on your Story. Updating your brochure? Describe the brand's Style to your designer. Writing a social media post? Remember your Voice. Bringing a partner or team member on board? Run them through the whole Canvas!

To make your Brand Canvas accessible, keep a copy on hand wherever you work. Save a version to your desktop, your phone, and the Cloud. Print a hard copy and paste it over your desk. If you'll be tempted to stress over the details and change it every five minutes, laminate it first.

Your brand will change over time, and so should your Canvas. I recommend sitting down to review your brand every six to twelve months. Think of it like a spring cleaning or changing the oil in your car. Schedule a few hours to review your Canvas (with partners or team members, if you have them). A lot happens in any business over six months. Whether you just need to make small tweaks or reflect major pivots, update your Brand Canvas thoroughly so it will be truly useful for the next six to twelve months.

Making this practice a habit will ensure you're building off all your hard work and developing a strong, healthy, thriving brand.

What's Next?

Congratulations! You're officially the expert on your brand. You can articulate who will fall in love with your brand, why your business exists, what your superpowers are, and how your brand looks and sounds. You've crafted a strong and strategic Brand Canvas.

It's time to build a brand that real humans love.

GLOSSARY

Behaviors: Actions and activities of your target customer that affect how your brand engages with them.

Brand: The unique identity of a business, guided by the business itself but ultimately existing in the minds of customers.

Brand Canvas: The one-page tool created by branding agency Sunbird Creative to capture a big-picture view of all the components of a small business brand.

Brand Guidelines: A set of rules that govern how a business portrays its brand identity, including style and voice.

Branding: The process of creating a consistent and unique brand identity.

Brand Persona: A description of the distinctive identity of a business as if it were a person with a specific role, traits, and intentions.

Core Competency: What a business does best.

Demographics: The kind of data about people you might find in a census, such as age and gender.

Differentiators: The qualities or characteristics that make one brand or product stand out from the rest.

Language Guide: Comprehensive guidelines that help make a

brand's voice human and consistent, including persona and tone.

Mission: The deeper reason a business does what it does.

Psychographics: Characteristics that describe how target customers think and feel, including attitudes and opinions.

Story: The narrative behind how a brand came to be and why it exists.

Style: A description of how a brand looks and feels.

Style Guide: Comprehensive guidelines that guide all design decisions for a brand and keep the brand's look and feel unique and consistent.

Target Customer: The type of person who is most likely to fall in love with a brand.

Unique Value Proposition: A short description of what makes a brand better than any other in the eyes of the target customers.

Value Proposition: An articulation of why a certain type of person would love a certain brand or product.

Values: Key principles that guide a business' decision-making.

Voice: The translation of a brand persona into the way a brand sounds, including tone.

FINAL NOTES

If you found this book helpful, please leave us a review on Amazon so other business owners have a better chance of finding this resource as well!

To download free Brand Canvas templates in multiple formats, visit sunbirdcreative.com/toolkits

If you are ready to create additional guidelines for your brand, including a Target Customer Profile, Language Guide, Style Guide, and Customer Journey Map — the Brand Identity Toolkit is perfect for you. Receive 50% off the Brand Identity Toolkit for being a reader with the code SMALLBIZLOVE. Find out more at sunbirdcreative.com/toolkits

ABOUT THE AUTHOR

Bianca van der Meulen is the co-founder and brand strategist at boutique agency Sunbird Creative. A clarity addict obsessed with making branding make sense, she's served hundreds of entrepreneurs through consultations, creative services, and education since 2012. She graduated summa cum laude from New York University and has taught branding classes at Union Settlement, Harlem Business Alliance, the International Center for Photography, and the Columbia-Harlem Small Business Development Center at Columbia University.

Made in the USA
Middletown, DE
01 December 2019

79787628R00076